INFLUENCE

INFLUENCE

*How social media influencers are
shaping our digital future*

SARA McCORQUODALE

BLOOMSBURY BUSINESS
LONDON · NEW YORK · OXFORD · NEW DELHI · SYDNEY

BLOOMSBURY BUSINESS
Bloomsbury Publishing Plc
50 Bedford Square, London, WC1B 3DP, UK
29 Earlsfort Terrace, Dublin 2, Ireland

BLOOMSBURY, BLOOMSBURY BUSINESS and the Diana logo are trademarks of
Bloomsbury Publishing Plc

First published in Great Britain 2019
This edition published in paperback 2021

ISBN: PB: 978-1-4729-7956-8
        ePDF: 978-1-4729-7200-2
        eBook: 978-1-4729-7199-9

Typeset by RefineCatch, Limited, Bungay, Suffolk
Printed and bound in Great Britain by CPI Group (UK) Ltd, Croydon CR0 4YY

2 4 6 8 10 9 7 5 3 1

To find out more about our authors and books visit www.bloomsbury.com
and sign up for our newsletters.

For Isabel
My greatest influence

CONTENTS

ACKNOWLEDGEMENTS

Writing this book has been one of the most fulfilling experiences of my career and not something that would have happened without the help and generosity of others. Primarily, the influencers I interviewed who were forthcoming about their experiences and understood this was an exploration of the good, bad and future of digital influence, and not simply an opportunity for self-promotion. While the majority spoke on the record, some felt unable to for fear of a backlash. Regardless of the circumstances in which we communicated, every conversation I've had about the influencer industry is in here somewhere, and everything I have written flows from what I learned from these people.

Also crucial to making this happen was my literary agent, Zoe King of A.M. Heath, who insisted I write the book that I believed the market needed, and that we find a publisher who supported this vision. Her encouragement from our earliest discussions made me certain I had to get this done, despite the fact I was in the middle of a truly awful pregnancy and working every hour to scale my business. It is hard to imagine a better person to have had on my side.

Speaking of publishers, Ian Hallsworth was the person I most wanted to work with, from our very first meeting. The fact he saw the benefit in businesses genuinely understanding the world of digital influence allowed me to approach this book journalistically rather than as a commentator. Writing a book that provides answers – as opposed to thoughts – on a relatively grey area was entirely down to his commitment to my original pitch. The whole team I worked with at Bloomsbury was endlessly supportive and inspiring and I am so proud that my book has been published by this company.

Given its subject, now seems a good opportunity to acknowledge the people who have influenced my journey which has led me to this point. Believe me, it took a village. My fascination in the intricacies of how people tell stories comes directly from the inspiring teachings of Linda McGlinchey and Adrian Hunter, who showed me how to be a better reader, writer and listener. Meanwhile, my understanding of influence and its power in a business context is one I learned from Kate Reardon during my time at *Tatler*. I will always be grateful to have worked for her as part of that team – it was truly the most enlightening year of my life.

It is unthinkable that I would be where I am without the support of Annabel Rivkin who I met at Condé Nast, and who encouraged me to pursue my own destiny rather than making money for other people. At a time when life was chaotic due to my oldest son being ill, she brought me into the fold of her business and taught me how to do everything better. She is the most generous, wise, clever person I know and, helpfully, always right. Through Annabel I met and worked for the amazing Rita Konig, who told me to start CORQ (and to call it CORQ). Her conviction that all of this would be successful was so persuasive, I went ahead and did it.

Over the past three years, I would have lost my mind had it not been for Emilie McMeekan. When I desperately needed to develop my business, she came onboard and elevated everything we do. Her empathy and intelligence has made my company feel like home for the entire team and her editorial genius is the thing that kept this book on the straight and narrow from day one. The entire CORQ team has contributed to this book and their ideas and insights have helped shape my own. Arabella Johnson, Chloe James, Jennifer Adetoro, Lucinda Diamond, Prue Lewington and Sunita Mahay – thank you for being the best, cleverest and coolest team in startup land.

Despite my many jobs (approximately 62) and experiences, the most impactful turning point in my career was Guy Baring becoming my mentor in 2016 and later, the first investor in my company. His guidance has been truly transformative and his understanding storytelling is at the heart of the influencer phenomenon, crucial. It is almost impossible to put in to words how much his support has changed my life.

Lastly, thank you to all the friends and family for sticking with me through writing this book, not to mention my ongoing career obsession. In particular, I would have been homeless/quit journalism numerous times since 2001 had it not been for the next level friendships of Carlene Thomas-Bailey, Sonia Cardoso, Kirsty Gallen, Urmee Khan, Francesca Young, Louise Boyle and Jennifer McVey. In every bad situation, I've been rescued by at least one of them. My parents-in-law, Diane and Tony, have offered kindness and help at every turn, and my parents – my stepfather, George, and my extraordinary mother, Isabel – have never lost faith in me or stopped encouraging me to try harder and think bigger.

To the person I share every day with – my husband and favourite friend, Simon – thank you for believing in the power of possibility, equal parenting and me.

And lastly, to my boy wonders, Dylan and Jonah – all of this is for you.

Introduction

Picture the scene. It is March 2020 and the whole world, it seems, is in lockdown thanks to the Covid-19 pandemic. The only way to fight the virus is to stay inside. Shops are shut and socialising is out of the question. So what do people do? They join TikTok and lip-synch, dance and skit their way out of self-isolation's boredom. The result? A whole new generation of stars are born in a single 12-week period. Welcome to the influencer industry, where speed and smartphone skills can lead to overnight fame – if you play your cards right.

The TikTokker is just the latest archetypal character of the social media landscape and joins an already established cast of YouTubers, Instagrammers, Twitch streamers and bloggers. Regardless of job title, they are all united by the fact that they have shaped the social media landscape, defined consumer expectations of digital entertainment and created the career now known as 'influencer'.

Regardless of their job title, they are a group of entrepreneurs who began with online diaries, make-up tutorials, comedic skits and goofy gaming vlogs. But over the past decade the emergent industry of digital influence has become a billion-dollar phenomenon that has smashed up the arenas of media, marketing and communication, and is forecast to continue growing exponentially. It started with YouTube content and earnest blogging, but these days influencers are being cast in films, transitioning to television and launching their own VC-backed businesses. And their audiences? They're buying in – evolving from passionate followers to loyal customers.

Brands, advertising agencies and media companies are falling over themselves to cosy up to these individuals and rightly so, because there is one thing that unites everyone currently holding this job title of influencer: they own the internet. They determine its direction, the style of content we watch, the things we buy, the thoughts in our head (to an extent). They are the shopping editors, broadcasters and opinion sharers we care about. Everyone wants a piece of the influence industry.

Rather than being an unexplainable fluke, as it is still dismissed in some more traditional quarters, this phenomenon occurred largely due to human behaviour. First, let's look at Facebook, which took the internet from being a place characterized by infinite information – things we didn't know – and turned it into a space about us. Our stories. Up until this point, online behaviour had centred around Google – our porthole to the wild, unknown, fantastical other. Everything could be learned and understood, quickly and easily. The world was suddenly much easier to grasp and travel, and information did not just belong to the universities, institutions and libraries but to everyone regardless of means, luck and education.

However, from approximately 2006 it began to satellite around us: our friends, family, thoughts, opinions and daily lives, in all their monotonous – yet addictively relatable – glory. It is strange to think that, once upon a time, it was unthinkable for most people to put pictures of themselves on the internet. As we became addicted to sharing our stories, so too did we become obsessed with other people's. They were the same, but different. Better, but attainable. By the time YouTube, Twitter and Instagram had exploded and social media had basically become the internet, consuming influencer content seemed more normal than sitting down to watch the BBC. One can fall into a black hole of TikTok content as easily as they can spend hours browsing Netflix.

But how has the industry ended up being worth so much? Why do brands need these people? Can't they just use social media and do what the influencers are doing too? In a word, no. The rise of the influencer means that, as consumers, we now have the expectation of a human lens on everything. A real storyteller with feelings and experiences that inform opinions they are willing to share in great detail. We don't want a brand voice. We don't want the 'royal we'. We don't want awkward marketing copy attempting to ape internet slang. Ironically, in this age of artificial intelligence – where technology has never been so advanced – we want human beings more than ever.

Add to this the fact that more than a quarter of people globally use adblocking software – meaning a huge number of consumers don't actually see the adverts brands have paid for on media websites – and hey presto! You have an industry. A really bloody valuable one. A brand can't be a person, but an influencer can. Essentially, theirs is the business of being human and telling stories about it.

Prior to starting my business, CORQ, in 2016, which is an independent influencer intelligence and digital trends platform, I was a journalist, editor and consultant for twelve years and my own journey is largely the reason I have written this book. I started working with influencers in 2012 to grow the online audiences first at *Tatler* and then for an AOL lifestyle website called MyDaily. Doing this with the former was easy – I became the magazine's first digital editor at the height of Channel 4 show *Made in Chelsea*'s popularity. A constructed reality programme – depicting the lives of young upper-class toffs in London – it was a godsend in terms of driving traffic to what was, at that point, a simple website with no hope of investment from Condé Nast unless I could prove consumer desire for what it had to offer. However, a core part of our offering was society party pictures and half of *Made in Chelsea*'s cast had already had galleries of their eighteenth birthday bashes published on our platform. When they joined the show, our content was more or less the only content about them available on the internet and fans – desperate to learn more about the stars – flooded to Tatler.com via Google. Partnering with them was just the next logical step and as a result *Tatler*'s digital audience grew exponentially in a short space of time. We had the right editorial, a captive audience who cared about young posh Brits, and young posh Brits who were happy to align themselves with the brand. Did I mention it was also the year of Queen Elizabeth II's Diamond Jubilee celebrations and the London 2012 Olympics? It was bingo, brilliant, the perfect storm.

MyDaily was a much trickier proposition. Its owner, AOL, valued numbers demonstrating high growth more than anything else as exponential page views and unique visitors would generate significant advertising revenue, right? Wrong. To deliver on targets, MyDaily's celebrity content – created for millennial women – was seeded on AOL's homepage, which was mostly visited by men who were in their thirties and older. As a result, our website had an unsolvable problem: it was aimed at women and being promoted to men, which resulted in it having an audience and context which appealed to no one. It was an impossible sell, yet corporate obsession with numbers over quality meant AOL homepage promotion – and thus the flow of men to MyDaily – continued. Adding to the problem was allegiance to a marketing program called Outbrain, which – for a price – seeded clickbait-style links to your content on popular websites across the internet to ensure large volumes of clickthrough and seeming audience growth. Again, the numbers looked impressive but the reality was grim. Outbrain delivered views, but no loyalty and our bounce rate (when users land on to a website and immediately leave again) was through the roof. On paper, MyDaily looked successful. In reality, it was all built on smoke and mirrors – we had no brand recognition and certainly no core, loyal audience. As editor, it was my job to change this – to bring millennial women to the website and make them love it – the way they loved Refinery29, Elite Daily and Buzzfeed. A key part of my strategy was hiring influencers to write our columns and be our photographers. They promoted their work on their social platforms, opened up their networks to us and gave us insight into what they liked. Suddenly, MyDaily was a little bit more interesting to its target market. Corporate obsession with volume at AOL made it pretty impossible to change things in a dramatic way, but the only thing that started to push the website in the right direction was our influencer strategy.

From there, I went to global trend forecaster WGSN to be a senior editor and one of my jobs was launching its first B2C website, WGSN Insider. Having inherited such a problematic brand in MyDaily, the idea of a box-fresh platform to which I could apply everything I'd learned in digital from – at that point – a decade in the business was a dream. If there was one thing I wanted for this new website, it was the right audience – designers, art students, creative directors; current and future customers returning again and again because it informed and represented them every single day. To do this, we produced a series of niche listicles ('10 things you only know if you studied textiles') and commissioned creative influencers to write guest blogs on everything from working with models in the 1990s to the genius behind the design of the Brompton bicycle. The content worked across newsletter, Twitter and Facebook, and was cross-promoted on contributors' social channels. It was like *Tatler* all over again.

If there's one thing that will inspire you to leap away from success and start your own business despite having absolutely no idea how to start your own business, it's being broke and having a sick baby whose bedtime you keep missing because you're always working. And that's why I left WGSN to be an independent consultant. Up until this point, I had commissioned influencers to essentially contribute to digital platforms I was charged with growing but in the first three months of moving into consultancy, I ended up being hired to grow the social audiences of two influencers' projects. One of these individuals was an international supermodel who had appeared on the covers of magazines, runways and billboards globally. Another was an independent creative who had significant authority in their field due to two decades spent demonstrating their ability through much-loved projects and coverage in print media. The former had over a million followers on Instagram and Facebook and it seemed to be a logical assumption that, through her cross-promoting her new project, growth would swiftly follow. However, the reality was her audience simply did not care. They wanted to see pictures of her and would like them in their droves, but she couldn't command them to do anything. She was entertaining but not influential.

Meanwhile, the creative started with a few thousand followers, grew rapidly and started to make money in a number of ways via Instagram within six months. The audience that accumulated was adoring, obedient and curious. They asked questions, praised the work of the influencer constantly and jumped at opportunities to attend their events and buy in to their brand on a greater scale. It was extraordinary – they trusted her authority and expertise implicitly and, due to this, she had significant influence. On the face of it, the supermodel was the more successful influencer, yet the reality was the creative was the only one of the two worthy of this title. At this point, I started to question the metrics upon which this emergent industry of digital influence were being judged. This was 2016, and mass was valued most. People had begun to talk about micro influencers but – again – this was defined by audience size and what constituted as 'micro' varied wildly.

The questions that had started to form in my head were these: do we have any reason to believe people with large social audiences have the power to influence their audiences beyond their number of followers and engagement rate? Are they influential or just popular? And is there any reason brands are associating with certain influencers beyond this numerical information and potentially an Instagram aesthetic which broadly reflects their own? As a journalist, you are taught to look for a hook. Unless the subject is someone or something which is continuously relevant, the hook is basically the reason why you would write about them at a specific moment in time. What have they done that aligns them to your publication and why should your reader care? I realized the thing missing from almost every influencer campaign was the hook. For example, this is when a content creator publishes a sponsored picture of them holding a bottle of perfume for no other reason than the fact they are being paid. Would a consumer buy into this just because it looked nice? Working with the supermodel had proved aesthetic was not enough; the thing that drove influence was authority, therefore the hypothetical content creator would require some level of knowledge in or at least a previously expressed love for fragrance and the brand behind it. The consumer must have a reason to trust them, to be influenced by their recommendation.

I realized that unless brands were much more deeply acquainted with influencers' stories, it would be impossible to produce meaningful influencer campaigns. There would never be a hook, a reason for consumers to buy in or believe the connection between them and the brand went beyond money. Without the hook, the influencer is just a gun for hire and the brand is a means to an end. Uncomfortable though it is, this is the reality of judging digital influence on numerical data alone. It is reductive for the content creators and significantly limits the potential of brands to capitalize on their abilities. The strength of the former party is rooted in their skill of telling stories and documenting their lives in a way that is aspirational or has cultural relevance – this is what makes them entertaining. But do their followers have any reason to trust their recommendation as far as your brand or industry goes? That is authority, which delivers trust, may translate into influence and then – the holy grail – conversion.

As the influencer space becomes more and more congested, it is easier than ever to scroll past generic, derivative content and therefore brand storytelling on social media must get better to ensure cut-through. It also must be believable. In my time as a consultant, I worked with many luxury brands globally and they are more attuned to this than those in any other sector. Natural believability of their brand in the influencer's context is crucial. Audience size is noted, but legacy and lifestyle are far more persuasive. This questioning of influencer legitimacy led me to build my platform CORQ and to dig into how an industry sprang up around these individuals. Why did it happen and what is it about its beginnings that has resulted in an extremely exciting but, also, extremely flawed space that people are still desperately trying to understand? Also, how did influencers build their brands? Were they simply early adopters who benefited from right place, right time, pre-algorithmic luck or did their wisdom go beyond that? The most significant thing that came out of many influencer interviews – some of which happened off the record – is the individuals themselves are dissatisfied with the industry that has emerged around them. In addition, they are almost unanimously uncomfortable with the term 'influencer' – it is neither one they created or use to describe themselves.

Broadly, they believe their value lies in their ability to build communities through consistent, relatable, authoritative and regular content. The relationship they have with their followers is often the thing they discuss most as it has taken time, and they have worked to build a trust and rapport. Also, just about every early adopter interviewed is keen to be less associated with the platforms upon which they built their names but it is possible their digital career will not stretch beyond these. Many of those YouTubers who built enormous followings there and on Instagram are finding that this audience is not going with them to TikTok. They want lifestyle advice and commentary, but have no interest in seeing these influencers learn an amusing dance to a viral tune.

On the other hand, the early adopting TikTokkers have grown their audiences at lightning speed. Following this success, they have crossed over to Instagram and their passionate TikTok followers? They have accompanied them, meaning the next generation of Instagram influencers are actually being born on TikTok.

Regardless of their preferred platform, it cannot be underestimated how significantly some have commodified their lives and stories and how aggressively they or their managers will defend this unless the price is right. Numerous influencers refused to be interviewed for this book on the grounds that they would not be paid for their time or their product. Their product is essentially their story. Some were also offended by the request, immediately suspicious that I was attempting to make money from their fame and success. Having spent many years building entertainment brands in a space that the majority of people did not value or understand, they are hypersensitive that those who ignored them – any traditional industry – now want to exploit them.

On the flipside, those who did want to talk spoke about the need for greater delineation in the industry – the word influencer is too broad to describe thousands of entrepreneurs, each building their own brand. Due to this, the influencers profiled in this book cover a broad spectrum of people telling different stories who have accumulated audiences and influence in different ways. YouTubers, Instagrammers, bloggers, creatives, commentators, authors and activists all make up the tapestry of the following chapters, which aims to demonstrate the depth of this industry, its flaws, potential and future. Full disclosure? At the end of a two-year research period, I believe individuals with digital influence have great power but I do not believe all people with significant social followings have great digital influence. I believe it is possible for brands to utilize influencers in a way that increases their relevancy and makes their products more appealing, but I do not believe this will necessarily result in widespread conversion. And ultimately, I believe all of this hinges on understanding human stories, as only then can we start to effectively achieve believability, trust and identify authority. This is the most plausible route to influence.

1

What is an influencer?

'Influencer' (noun): an individual who has built a digital audience through sharing editorialized content about their life.

Why did the influencer industry happen?

Influencer. A term that is desired and loathed, both by those working with people who hold the title and the individuals themselves. It has many negative connotations – freeloader being the most prevalent one – but, in truth, those who deserve the title (and not everyone who has it does) are entrepreneurs who have not only created a digital entertainment landscape worth billions but who also dictate where it is going next. Why? Because of the significant, captive audiences they have built, who follow their every move and thought across multiple social platforms.

Rightly or wrongly interchangeable with the titles content creator, blogger, Instagrammer and YouTuber, the word influencer is symbolic of a new kind of media mogul – one who is independent, industrious and has capitalized on their online popularity to launch further creative projects and successful startups. Their strengths include being able to adapt nimbly to the ever-evolving digital environment, identifying and acting upon opportunities that will result in further growth of their brands and, ultimately, understanding what makes their audiences tick. Their weaknesses? Buying too heavily into their own hype and being so deeply attuned to the culture they have created within their own platforms that they are entirely out of touch with what is acceptable within a wider cultural narrative.

Although it feels ubiquitous with the language of marketing, media, digital and communications now, the term itself – 'influencer' – is one that has entered our vocabulary gradually. According to Google data, minimal searches containing the word started towards the end of 2013 and began to gather notable pace in 2017, sharply rising through 2018. In the second half of the latter year, there was no significant dip in the term's popularity and over that five-year period people searching for the word most were in Singapore, Germany and Switzerland. There were also hundreds of thousands of queries for 'influencer' coming from America – particularly in New York, California and Utah – and the UK.

The precursor to the term was the more succinct and less problematic title 'blogger', and it is worth noting that online searches for this are globally and exponentially larger than those for 'influencer'. The latter is industry vernacular – essentially, a made-up word to explain a media phenomenon at elevator-pitch speed – and the problems attached to the emergent sector of influencer marketing can largely be traced to the inaccurate connotations suggested by the job title of influencer itself.

However problematic the term may be, lack of understanding has not stopped an industry funded by brands and agencies from springing up around YouTubers, Instagrammers and cross-platform content creators. Valued at an estimated $2bn in 2017, it is forecast to be worth five times this by 2020 and has quickly accumulated astonishing value, arguably due to uncertainty about where advertising and media are going in the age of digital. Condé Nast UK reported a pre-tax loss of £13.6m in 2017 – something the publisher attributes to its investment in online growth – while Hearst suffered an 8 per cent decline in circulation in 2018. Meanwhile, the majority of print titles across the board saw a continuing trend of dipping sales, according to ABC figures.

In tandem, advertising revenue for print titles has also slowed (although there was a slight upturn for newspapers in 2018), with brands preferring to strike 'partnerships' with magazines and newspapers, rather than invest heavily in traditional display propositions. These deals often involve an array of sponsored content across print and digital, alongside presence at events, social media promotion and access to starry editors, who, in many cases, are influencers in their own right. Why not simply move advertising spend from print properties to their websites? After all, the latter tend to have much bigger readerships and daily publishing schedules across several platforms. Yet thanks to ad-blocking software – utilized by approximately one quarter of all internet users – digital display advertising is no guarantee that the millions of people visiting websites will actually see the adverts on them.

The difficulties in funding online media have manifested in staff cuts and devaluations across several digital news brands that were once thought to be the future of the industry. In 2019, Buzzfeed announced plans to lay off 15 per cent of its global workforce, and Verizon revealed it would cull 7 per cent of its headcount across HuffPost, AOL and Yahoo. It also took a \$4.6bn write-down on its valuation in 2018, and Vice Media shared plans to reduce its team by 15 per cent. Meanwhile, viral publisher UNILAD went into administration in 2018, as did UK women's lifestyle website The Pool the following year. At a time when Twitter was awash with journalists and editors announcing they had been made redundant, *Spears* magazine estimated Zoe Sugg's net worth at £2.5m. YouTuber Olajide Olatunji – better known as KSI – was reported to be worth £3.9m and fellow vlogger Logan Paul £11m.

Anyone in the position of communications and marketing heads, media planners and brand directors is being tasked with ensuring awareness remains high, sales grow year-on-year and their product is relevant to core and future markets. While established traditional brands must meet aggressive targets and be seen as industry leaders, startups and emergent competitors must be challengers and ensure their brand is where people are actually spending time online. And where are these people? On social media. Not necessarily following brands, but actively choosing to be part of communities built by influencers who inform, entertain, listen to and facilitate timely conversations for them.

While traditional media has seen print sales decline and digital propositions flounder, the majority of mainstream Western social platforms have continued to grow. Most notable is Instagram, which doubled from having 500 million monthly users in 2017 to 1 billion in 2018, and even Facebook – which dealt publicly with several controversies over its commercialization of users' data – amassed millions of new users during this time. However, despite platform growth there has been widespread reporting on a decline in the efficiency of direct advertising on social platforms. Most notably, Facebook's algorithm change in 2018 – which prioritized interactions between people in users' newsfeeds over posts from brands and publishers – has been disastrous for those trying to reach eyeballs with campaigns. Meanwhile, Instagram's newsfeed changed from being chronological to being ordered by engagement. So, yes, while people are on social platforms in their millions, reaching them with brand content has become much more difficult. Essentially, the solution to this problem for brands and agencies is to find a human conduit – in other words, an influencer.

For social platforms, brand and agency money going directly into influencers' pockets instead of theirs is also problematic. In direct influencer marketing, the platforms are cut out of the relationship entirely and YouTube, Facebook, Instagram and Twitch have made efforts to nurture relationships with content creators to ensure they remain part of the picture. Not only have they seen consumers' appetite for what these people can do – from bloggers to traditional celebrities – but it appears to be clear to them the future of their businesses is rooted in entertainment led by influencers. They can sell advertising and sponsorship deals here and, despite algorithm changes aimed at addressing the demands of their userbase, still make money.

What do influencers actually do? What is their appeal?

Who are these people, what do they do and what does this term mean? The definition that opens this chapter is the closest and clearest way of describing how the role of the influencer is broadly understood, although in truth influencers are simply independent media brands who excel in covering one thing deeply: their own lives. While many opt to share everything across multiple platforms on a daily basis – what they wear, eat, think, make – others create content showing what they do, for example gaming or crafting, and publish this alongside less frequent snippets of personal information.

Take the Venn diagram in Figure 1. As you can see, one circle is labelled celebrity and overlaps with a second, labelled media. The space occupying the overlap is the place in which the influencer exists. Like traditional media, they share information; unlike traditional media, it is all from a personal perspective.

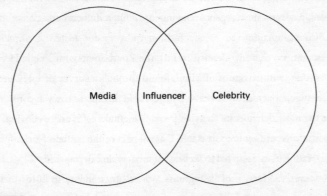

Media Influencer Celebrity

FIGURE 1

And, like celebrities, their followers – their fans – aspire to their lifestyle, but unlike celebrities their lives are presented as relatable and achievable. That's it in a nutshell for influencers working across YouTube and Instagram.

Meanwhile, Twitter is a different proposition used best by influencers who are skilled at commenting on current affairs strongly, humorously and quickly. The appeal here is not that their followers want to emulate their lives but that they want to be part of or watch the conversations they prompt, which they are able to do faster and much more fervently than any traditional news brand. This is why many of the most prominent influencers on Twitter are newspaper columnists, broadcasters and media commentators – they are close to current affairs and it is, in fact, their job to have an opinion on them.

Regardless of the platforms on which they are most prolific, influencers' ability to speak directly to their followers and publish regularly and reactively allows them to be continual and reliable presences in their audiences' lives. They share achievements, admit mistakes and document the mundane. The attention they pay to the relatable nitty-gritty and smallness of everyday life – as well as milestone moments – gives their followers the impression they have a direct line to them. This is not curated media but real-time stream of thought and broadcasting.

The exception to this is Instagram. Lifestyle influencers' tendency to portray perfection during the first era of the platform has been the catalyst for hundreds of think pieces on the dangers of buying into a filtered documentation of life. It has also been compared to the fashion industry for fostering unrealistic representations of body identity. In fact, the Royal Society for Public Health's 2017 survey, entitled Status of Mind, found through a survey of 1,479 people aged between fourteen and twenty-four years old that Instagram was considered to be the most detrimental thing to people's mental health and wellbeing. The organization's resultant report stated that users' 'compare and despair' response to the platform's content led to feelings of anxiety and depression.

However, the launch of Instagram's Stories functionality in 2016 – which allowed users to publish ad hoc-style imagery and video that stays live for just twenty-four hours – has led to influencers changing how they use the platform. While their permanent content on the grid remains curated and filtered, their Stories are often grittier and used to discuss personal crises, topical issues and show a more realistic side of their lives. As Clemmie Telford – founder of website Mother of All Lists, Instagram parenting influencer and ex-Facebook employee – says, Instagram launched Stories to 'puncture the perfectly curated feed and so that people would use the platform more like a diary'. She adds: 'There's nothing wrong with having content that's long-lasting, but this gave the platform an extra, more real layer.'

This 'real layer' is crucial to influencers' success, particularly for those aiming to build a community rather than something more akin to an aspirational look-book, simply documenting their aesthetic and the products they have used to create it. Influencers sharing raw experiences and struggles – from heartbreaking rounds of IVF treatment to mental health issues and financial difficulties – catalyse larger conversations and give their followers the green light to talk about similar experiences. Telford's decision to share her husband's business going bankrupt resulted in an outpouring from women also facing financial crises. Since then, she has documented her experience of marriage therapy and maternal mental health, and says her decision to be this transparent with her audience comes from her goal to portray life with a 'foundation of honesty'. Referring to her bankruptcy announcement in 2017, she says: 'During the actual crisis I wasn't ready to talk about it. But when I did, I found it was like everything I'd written about that is topical – you never know what others are going through and the people who relate are the last people who you think are going through the same thing as you.' She adds: 'Everyone has this constructed idea of the kind of person who would go bankrupt and you forget it can happen to anyone.' On the equally fervent response to her admission that she and her husband were in therapy, she says: 'I didn't expect it to be so important. The thing is, my husband and I are happy but it's a marriage. You can be in paradise and still fighting.'

While some influencers create spaces for discussion through publicly embracing the 'real layer' and sharing their greatest challenges, others do this through inviting their followers into the most private and personal experiences of their lives. These tend to be milestone events – weddings, births and break-ups. For example, when Los Angeles YouTuber and comedienne Colleen Ballinger – known as Miranda Sings – and fellow vlogger Joshua Evans decided to divorce in 2016, ending their eight-year relationship, she revealed the news on YouTube. 'I have always shared everything in my life with you guys and you've been a big part of my relationship with Josh,' she said. 'You deserve to know what's going on.' Fast forward to 2018, and Ballinger revealed she was pregnant with her new partner Erik Stocklin and later vlogged her labour.

Meanwhile, London lifestyle vlogger Patricia Bright and her husband Mike published a video of the former giving birth to their daughter Grace on YouTube in 2016. This involved an ambulance ride, the labour process and her emotional birth, after which she prays and Mike cuts the umbilical cord. From the hospital ward, Mike says to camera: 'This is without doubt, the happiest, happiest moment of my life.' At the time of writing this, over 1.8 million people had tuned in to watch the video. Birth vlogs are in no way unusual in the context of influencers. In fact, YouTuber Emily Norris took sharing this personal moment one stage further by being the first woman in the UK to broadcast her labour with her third son on Facebook Live in 2016.

Documentation of daily life – including milestones – produces linear narratives in which influencers' audiences can continually get involved, as this content is either highly relatable or elicits strong emotions. Nothing is omitted, and there are no gaps in the storyline. However, documentation of the 'real layer' is also good for business. Influencers' transparency creates a dynamic which is more akin to friendship than the one between a fan and a celebrity or a consumer and a traditional media brand, because the follower and the influencer are able to have a two-way, human conversation. Which brings us to another key part of what an influencer actually does – they close the feedback loop.

Thanks to the comments sections on every platform they publish across, followers' observations can be addressed by influencers almost immediately. This proximity means influencers' value not only lies in the content they create but in their ability to engage with their audience after publishing it. In a way, the content is just the start of the story and this conversation means they can develop relationships with their audiences in a way that feels personal but would be impossible for a brand or celebrity. While the former is constrained by communication guidelines, tone of voice restrictions and a sign-off process more suitable for the slower-paced traditional media, it is unlikely the latter could ever respond to every fan. Also, for some celebrities – let's say those at Beyoncé Knowles-Carter's level of fame – it is in their interest to maintain a degree of mystery.

Therefore, from a commercial perspective, influencers give brands a closeness to their consumers that they would be unable to achieve through their own platforms. Unlike brands and celebrities, sharing detail, cultivating community and updating their followers are influencers' primary purpose – in fact, it is possibly the most crucial function of their job, particularly when they are trying to grow. They answer comments, share their email addresses to encourage deeper interaction and make content in response to critiques or requests from their audiences.

Interestingly, some lifestyle influencers also use different platforms to capitalize on and showcase different aspects of their character. For example, a common strategy adopted by male lifestyle vloggers is to focus on comedic, food and conversational content for YouTube, while Instagram is dedicated to fashion and styling editorial. Meanwhile, they are more topical and reactive to current affairs on Twitter, expressing their political stance, encouraging their followers to vote or even just passing comment on television programmes. Comparatively, their presence here has more edge and has been the place they are likely to be most spontaneous. First, because it lends itself to this style of content, and second, because there are fewer commercial opportunities. Basically, they are under less pressure to be brand-friendly on Twitter. However, with the uncovering of unsavoury historic tweets damaging several high profile influencers' brands, it is almost certain this looseness will increasingly disappear. For example, Zoe Sugg received widespread criticism when homophobic and classist tweets she had posted between 2009 and 2012 were discovered in 2017. Meanwhile, Kevin Pena – also known as Brother Nature – decided to make his Twitter account private for a period of time when historic misogynistic and anti-Semitic tweets he had published between 2011 and 2012 were uncovered. Both influencers pleaded young age and ignorance as a defence and were able to get back to business as usual fairly quickly. However, for others the re-emergence of historic tweets has had a much more detrimental impact commercially. Take Amena Khan, who decided to quit L'Oréal's influencer beauty squad in 2018 after tweets she posted in 2014 in which she criticized Israel's war in Gaza were uncovered. The beauty brand announced that it supported this decision.

Influencers tapping into different sides of their personalities for each social channel reflects what it takes to be numerically and commercially successful on each. For example, Instagram has been the ideal place to develop a polished, fashion- or lifestyle-focused aesthetic, which plays to steadily increasing brand budgets in these industries for producing glossy magazine-style campaigns for the platform. Meanwhile, YouTube requires high energy, quirky humour and apparent honesty combined with the act of 'experiencing', whether that means trying on a lipstick or going on a road trip. Developing different but broadly consistent personas, looks and narratives for each platform allows influencers to efficiently monetize their brands across the board and create a cohesive content plan, rather than trying to fit multiple styles of editorial into one space.

How do influencers make money?

This brings us to how influencers have commercialized their content. In terms of what they do and how they make money, their trajectories and business models vary. Some were early adopters of blogging and YouTube, before adding Twitter and Instagram to their repertoire, and have monetized their platforms through brand partnerships, creating sponsored content, hosting events and using affiliate links through which they receive a small commission if consumers buy product online having discovered it via influencer channels. Vloggers can also receive payment from YouTube, the size of which is related to advertising revenue and how many times their videos are watched. Meanwhile, streaming platform Twitch – which is best known for influencers live broadcasting themselves playing video games – allows viewers to pay a subscription fee, part of which goes directly to the content creator. However, this payment by the viewer is largely philanthropic as it is possible to watch Twitch content free of charge.

The greatest criticism of influencer modes of making money is centred around how paid promotion of products and places via content on their social channels impacts on their authenticity, given documentation of the 'real layer' and a seeming lack of commercial agenda, is the very reason their audience bought in to them in the first place. This is also what made influencer platforms appealing alternatives to traditional media brands, whose commercial deals with brands inevitably effect editorial content. For example, it is in a magazine's interest to promote a certain product in its features pages if the brand has advertised elsewhere in the publication but – in the beginning – influencers were simply sharing things they had found to be useful to help their followers. Commercialization of platforms has tested the influencer and follower dynamic and led to the former adopting an increasingly transparent approach to signposting products they have bought, been given by brands or been paid to promote. Indeed, the UK's Competitions and Markets Authority made it mandatory for influencers to disclose not only if they were promoting brands because they had been paid to do so, but also if they had ever worked with said brands before, even on non-sponsored content.

Despite this, the fact they are making money via product promotion is a major turn-off and something their followers can be heavily critical of. There is also a degree of disbelief from influencers' audiences if they promote a product or brand that they think the influencer would be unlikely to produce content about if they were not being paid to do so. For example, an Instagram post in 2018 by Alfie Deyes promoting a Daniel Wellington watch was scoffed at by one of his followers, who commented: 'He's got a Cartier bracelet. Can't see him wearing a Daniel Wellington one over that.'

However, is this legitimate criticism, given traditional media brands have been funding their operations in this manner for decades? Holiday resort reviews by travel editors are often the result of all-expenses-covered press trips organized by PR agencies, tour operators and hotel groups while – as already mentioned – advertisers also feature heavily in publications' editorial content. If consumers accept this from newspapers and magazines, why not from influencers? There are two reasons. First, influencers are still seen as people and ultimately expected to behave in this way. They are yet to be widely regarded as independent media brands – despite this being their function. Second, the commercialization of influencer platforms shines a light on the uncomfortable reality of the relationship between an influencer and their audience: the latter's devotion allows the former to make money. Regardless of how it is framed and despite significant interaction, theirs is not a friendship and the entire construct exists for business reasons. For example, under Colleen Ballinger's aforementioned videos documenting the birth of her son, she promotes her range of lipstick. Influencers provide entertainment and the illusion of friendship, but that is their job. While one unquestioningly accepts advertising from a faceless media brand, it is more difficult to swallow when it comes from an individual.

However, sponsored content is not the only way influencers generate income from their audiences. They have diverged into traditional media too, having secured book deals, radio presenting slots and television work, the logic behind this being if they can bring their substantial audience from new to old media, the latter will be in a significantly better position. For example, Zoe Sugg's first book, *Girl Online*, was the fastest selling book of 2014 and her non-fiction hardback on entertaining, *Cordially Invited*, was a bestseller in 2018, despite being widely criticized for its simplicity (it instructed readers to use umbrellas in the rain). Meanwhile, fellow YouTuber Alfie Deyes' Pointless Book series accounted for £3.9m in sales in 2017. Sugg's younger brother Joe was a finalist in BBC show *Strictly Come Dancing* in 2018 and has since gained more work in terrestrial television. Achieving success in the realms of traditional media is a common influencer ambition. YouTuber Eman Kellam made his name through a video of him pranking his father, which went viral, but his ultimate goal is to host a late-night show for a US network.

Ironically, as traditional media companies desperately try to adapt their strategies and content to grow new audiences on digital platforms, the people who shaped these platforms – the influencers themselves – are turning to traditional media for opportunities that will validate their talent and pay them in a more straightforward manner. For many, social media is a means to an end – a way to reach the mainstream – and for those already there, from celebrities to models and even newspaper editors, there is increasing pressure to build social audiences.

On top of producing content, many influencers also run businesses and develop products whose success is made possible by their adoring social media audiences. This is most lucrative in instances where the influencer is so widely followed that they have achieved something akin to celebrity status. Their audience behaves more like ardent fans and collectors, believing it is crucial that they experience every part of the influencer's output and immediately share this on their own social channels. Being part of these influencer communities is a key element of their online identity – something they reference in their own biographies on Instagram and Twitter. In response to this, the influencer gives their followers a collective name to use. This is especially prominent on YouTube – vloggers The Ingham Family encourage their audience to be part of and use #iFAM.

It is the fervent loyalty of influencers' core audiences that makes the success of their ventures outside of social platforms plausible. While many have developed or co-created products and businesses in industries which they cover in their digital content, others use their fame to explore separate interests and launch new talent. YouTuber and podcaster Marcus Butler's signing of musician Maisie Peters to his entertainment management company, Stripped Bear, has been integral to her success as a breakthrough artist whose music is now streamed millions of times every month on Spotify. Through backing her publicly, his audience also felt compelled to show support to her and did so through downloading her music, following her on Instagram and watching her videos on YouTube.

Why is the term 'influencer' misleading?

The problem with the word 'influencer' is it assumes that apparent digital popularity – audience size, likes and comments – is evidence of an individual's ability to actually impact on consumer behaviour. It quantifies people engaging with online content as a sign they will act upon an influencer's suggestions; in reality, following someone, liking their content and even commenting on it is a relatively small commitment. If an individual has built a community in which their followers interact with them and each other, this indicates they have successfully created a strong enough narrative that others feel comfortable to share their own story in the context of this individual's. This can be both powerful and valuable, as it transforms the influencer's platforms into digital destinations for the people who are part of this community. They offer a sense of belonging.

However, it doesn't necessarily mean the influencer has the ability to convert any of those followers into customers for a brand. As mentioned previously, they risk destabilizing the trusted space they have created by attempting to sell products on their platforms. Hugo Rifkind, a columnist for *The Times* with tens of thousands of followers on Twitter, is uncomfortable with the term influencer. He says: 'Just because I have these followers doesn't mean I can get anybody to buy my book or anyone else's. I can't really leverage Twitter – and believe me, I've tried.'

YouTuber and author Louise Pentland admits her goal with her content is communication – not influence – while fashion blogger and author Katherine Ormerod believes the term influencer dehumanizes the individuals working in the industry. 'We aren't robots, as much as people want to reduce us to conversion rates,' she says.

She is also concerned the job title is too broad a term to be desirable or useful. 'I do think there will be further delineation,' she says. 'There are people who are more focused on generating sales with their content and those who are approaching it from a marketing perspective. These are two different jobs.' She adds: 'We're a generation of multi-hyphenates, although no one knows quite what to call us yet.'

Meanwhile, Clemmie Telford thinks the word itself disrupts the nature of the relationship between the content creator and their audience. 'I hate it – it suggests that we're somehow above people when actually you want to be peer-to-peer.'

Lifestyle blogger and Instagrammer Ramona Jones agrees. She says: 'It puts you in a hierarchy and makes it sound like you're at the top when actually your fate is completely in the hands of your following.'

In order for influencers to have the ability to sell product or raise awareness in a way that would result in return on investment, brands must be able to do two things. First, identify the root of these individuals' influence – be it parenting, dating, food. In what area have they achieved the absolute trust of their audience? Second, ensure the demographic that engages with this root is appropriate for the product they are attempting to market.

The idea that influencer channels could easily be commercialized is symptomatic of a widespread misunderstanding of the purpose of social media. While marketers and brands may want them to sell product, the truth is they exist to entertain, communicate and inform – essentially, to tell and interact with stories. Sales may be a by-product of this entertainment and information, but they cannot and will not happen unless the influencer can first deliver at least one of these elements successfully and brilliantly. In addition, it will be impossible for the influencer to achieve this repeatedly if they do not have a core audience that has remained loyal to them and has invested in the entirety of their story. The longer they have followed the influencer, the more certain they will be about whether or not they can be trusted as a source of information.

The second issue with current assumptions about the role of influencers is that they are influencing their followers en masse. In actual fact, there is a difference between being a digital celebrity and authoritative influence – while the former is primarily a source of entertainment, the latter has gained the trust and devotion of their followers due to proven expertise.

ANATOMY OF A DIGITAL CELEBRITY

THE PURPOSE OF THIS INFLUENCER is to share their lives – that is their full-time job. They exist to tell their story and have capitalized on the very fact that no one can do this as expertly as they can. Individuals consume this content as they would television – they are enthralled by the narratives, the relationships, what is going to happen next. Viewing the content of a digital celebrity is similar to watching that of a reality show – its power lies in the conversations between the protagonists and the fact the events are happening in familiar, if slightly elevated, circumstances. However, while reality television shows are edited to ensure viewers see the most pivotal and climactic moments of the different 'characters'' lives, digital celebrities may share lengthy vlogs every day covering everything from doing the dishes to going to the grocery store. Their output is more like a daily feed where, as discussed, the 'real layer' is key, rather than shocking viewers with high drama.

Take, for example, family YouTube channels through which regular families document their everyday lives. It might seem logical for a child-focused brand to form a commercial partnership with such a content creator, yet, by and large, the majority of these channels' subscribers tend to be teenagers. They are not watching for inspiration on how to manage family life but to be entertained by the family itself, therefore regarding their millions of subscribers as potentially millions of well-targeted consumers would be an error.

While digital celebrities can sell out lines of their own branded merchandise, it can be much more difficult for them to send consumers to a commercial partner. Prior to approaching a digital celebrity, one must ascertain what portion of their audience is consuming their content as entertainment – this tends to be the majority demographic – and the percentage of their following which is actually likely to require products related to their narrative.

ANATOMY OF THE AUTHORITATIVE INFLUENCER

THIS IS AN INDIVIDUAL WITH proven expertise who has gained a significant audience due to being a trusted authority in the space they are covering. This person may not share a significant amount of intimate information on their channels but this is not to their detriment. While warts-and-all is the currency of the digital celebrity, the authoritative influencer exists to inform their followers about products they recommend, trends, their latest projects and inspiration. They are beacons of good taste and also give their audiences the tools to ape their ability and style. Their influence often has significant legacy with them either having established themselves in their industry prior to the rise of social media or having shown themselves to be a trustworthy source of information as early adopters of social platforms.

Take interior designer and author Rita Konig, who made her name writing about design for *Vogue*, *Domino* and *The Wall Street Journal*, and assisting her mother, the equally influential interior designer Nina Campbell. She did this prior to launching her own studio, building a significant Instagram audience, launching an online store and a series of transatlantic workshops. Her audience is so influenced by her suggestions, so trusting of her authority, that Instagram has become a successful sales channel. She also has a column in *House & Garden* magazine and operates with one foot in traditional media and another firmly in digital. This combination of personal history in the interiors industry, a visible journey towards her current success and respected publications showcasing and endorsing her work has resulted in a brand of influence that is affectionate, authoritative and unquestionable.

THE OVERLAP

THAT IS NOT TO SAY an individual cannot encompass both digital celebrity and authoritative influence, but brands must again be fully informed of where these individuals' influence actually lies. If their authoritative influence is born out of years spent blogging and vlogging about a specific area – and their audience continues to engage heavily with their work – there is evidence their followers will trust their expertise. Although they may share significant details about their personal life, this kind of influencer has a clear specialism in which their audience has placed faith. Brands keen to commercialize on this should do so if their product is related to this area of expertise – this has clear potential to yield results. Consider Jack Harries' move from publishing travel vlogs on his YouTube channel, JacksGap, to producing content which exists to raise awareness of environmental issues – most prominently climate change. His actions over a sustained period of time back up his dedication to this cause – he is vegan, supports and promotes businesses in the vegan industry, and protests at demonstrations organized by environmental movements such as Extinction Rebellion. He uses his social platforms to share content about very little other than climate change and his followers now engage more with this messaging than they do with anything else he publishes.

Unless they have established their authority, partnering with influencers on new ventures in adjacent industries is much more risky and should be considered experimental. Take vlogger Tanya Burr, who has been publishing lifestyle content on YouTube since 2009 and, as a make-up artist by trade, specialized in beauty. She has amassed an audience of millions and shared everything – from having period pain to dealing with anxiety – with her followers across several platforms. She has also covered her ambition to become an actress, the training she has undertaken and updates on her progress. Yet when she made her stage debut in a 2018 London production of Judy Upton's play *Confidence*, produced by theatre company Boundless, the show did not sell out. It received poor reviews and resulted in numerous think pieces about the validity of 'stunt' casting to generate theatre ticket sales. While Burr's online star can maintain the attention of thousands, it seems it cannot yet persuade her audience to follow her off the internet and into an arena in which she is less established.

However, it seems any change of context can be a major turn-off for influencers' audiences, and it needn't be as dramatic as moving them offline. Comedy YouTuber Grace Helbig has millions of subscribers and therefore, when she was offered a late-night show by E!, it seemed on the surface like a smart way to attract an existing large audience to the channel, particularly as the programme promised to be similar to her YouTube content. On this occasion, however, Helbig's followers did not follow – they wanted her entertainment in the context of her living room, not a television set. After eight episodes, the show was cancelled.

The upshot of this chapter is that the initial definition of an influencer remains. An influencer is someone who has built an engaged audience around digital content about their lives. However, this title and word should be thought of as a noun rather than a verb or absolute description of the individual's function. Yes, one can recognize through numerical engagement – likes, comments and audience size – that a person described as an influencer is popular online and that their followers are entertained by their content. But, it does not necessarily mean they have the ability to turn anyone a customer. Popularity is not the same as influence; providing entertainment is not the same as having authority. Influence is much more difficult to quantify than the current metrics upon which influencers are judged might suggest. Early adopter of blogging and social media Susie Lau, founder of website Style Bubble, succinctly hit the nail on the head in a 2011 interview with *Business of Fashion*. When asked what exactly it was that she was selling to brands she partnered with, she said: 'It's intangible.' Despite numerous technology developers producing solutions which claim to predict and measure influence, this remains true.

KEY TAKEAWAYS

- The title 'influencer' is shorthand for people who have turned themselves into independent media companies. Although some can have an impact on the sales of certain brands, the majority have created their platforms to entertain and inform. The power to influence consumer behaviour may follow this if they have the trust of their audience, but it is in no way guaranteed.
- The influencer industry happened because consumers have gravitated away from traditional media to social platforms and chosen to follow individuals documenting their lives, rather than seeking inspiration and information from newspapers, magazines and established publishing brands. They chose fast-paced, interactive communities over a singular, authoritative voice.
- A changing digital landscape has made it much harder to reach consumers via online display advertising. More than one quarter of all internet users have installed ad-blocking software, while the notorious Facebook algorithm change of 2018 prioritized content by individuals over that published by brands. The upshot? Information coming from a human was more likely to be seen.
- The term 'influencer' is disliked by those to whom it is given for two main reasons. First, it suggests a hierarchical structure in which the influencer is more powerful than their followers – something that the influencers themselves argue is inaccurate. Second, it is simply too broad and does not recognize that there are people in the space doing vastly different things. It effectively flattens a market which is vibrant thanks in part to how diverse it is.
- Rapid commercialization and growth of the influencer industry has led to strict advertising guidelines being imposed by various industry bodies

who believe consumers are not sufficiently aware that, on numerous occasions, influencers are being paid to promote brands to them.

- This commercialization via sponsored content, affiliate links and promotional work threatens to destabilize the influencer/follower relationship as it highlights that, although this may feel like friendship to the latter, it is a business situation to the former.
- To a large extent, influencers' audiences follow and subscribe to their content for entertainment. They consume their work as one would television. These influencers tend to have mass audiences and are digital celebrities.
- Authoritative influencers are people who have a defined legacy and expertise in the area they are covering on their channels. Their audience trusts their judgement and this makes their function arguably more influential than that of a digital celebrity.

2

How did they do it?

They had no budget and few resources, yet they managed to leapfrog brands and traditional publishers to build enormous, loyal audiences across several platforms. So how did influencers do it? And what strategies did the successful ones employ to ensure their brands had longevity?

First of all, it is worth noting that the most prolific influencers were early adopters of blogging and vlogging, and started independently creating content that documented their lives and interests between 2004 and 2012, when the internet was a much less crowded space. In 2005, for example, approximately 14 million blogs were live. By 2010, there were 133 million and as of January 2019 there were 456 million on Tumblr alone. The internet is a vastly different landscape now – noisy, congested and sprawling – meaning early adopters who started publishing in the noughties without doubt had a better chance of making it as independent content creators. Never underestimate the power of being in the right place at the right time.

But their success was not simply down to a lack of competition and being ahead of the curve. The fact they have been sharing information about their lives for a much longer time than, say, content creators who emerged in the 2014–15 Instagram influencer boom means they have a much stronger legacy. Their audiences have been invested in their lives as viewers perhaps since they were teenagers. It is plausible they have gone through milestones together – whether those be university, relationships, or career failures and triumphs. Yet it's more than that. Review the content of any of these early independent publishers and it is possible to identify key tactics that kept their audiences coming back for more. These are the six guiding principles which allowed them to flourish online and turn a hobby into a career.

1   Bootstrapping a brand

To bootstrap means to use existing resources and apply a do-it-yourself, do-it-quickly philosophy in order to progress. For the early influencers, this meant WordPress and Blogger websites supplemented, in some cases, by YouTube channels for which they borrowed family cameras to make poorly edited videos. Consciously or subconsciously, they had decided to build brands using the bare minimum and relying – above everything else – on their personalities to ensure readers and viewers felt enough of a connection to their work that they would keep reading, watching and returning.

The result? Crudely produced, amateur-looking content littered with spelling mistakes, blurry pictures and inconsistencies. However, this was completely in keeping with the character of the internet at the time – pre-Instagram and without the high standard of smartphone cameras we have now, perfection was not an expectation of regular people digitally sharing their lives.

Also, these early adopters were not trying to compete with traditional media nor, at least initially, to play to the crowd. Everything they published was related to their personal ambitions to be bloggers or vloggers and communicate with their peers, and therefore this content was rooted in the things they did, liked and had. For Olivia Purvis – who founded What Olivia Did in 2010 – that initial tendency to always incorporate the personal into whatever she is writing or vlogging about is still part of her editorial plan. She says: 'My blog has always been very much what I'm interested in, and content that hopefully has some kind of takeaway value to the reader.'

These early blogs and YouTube channels portray the influencers as relatable, likeable individuals but did not signal future greatness. Australian blogger and entrepreneur Elle Ferguson started her website in 2007 and used it to publish moodboard-like posts featuring fashion she loved. 'Imagine a giant collage,' she says. 'It was daily inspiration from around the world.'

It's also worth noting that this was pre-selfie and, while these websites often featured professionally shot pictures from magazines, blogs were yet to become mines of personal style. In fact, Lucy Nicholls – who founded her website Shiny Thoughts in 2009 – didn't feature pictures of herself at all in the beginning. 'I just covered things like going to craft events and Graduate Fashion Week,' she says.

Esther Coren launched her website in 2007 and remembers that self-publishing had become something of an emergent trend. 'Everyone else seemed to have a blog, so I thought I'd start one, too,' she says. 'It was about teaching myself how to cook and I wrote it for seven years.'

There is a vast gulf between the homespun editorial of the noughties and the filtered and flawless content published by influencers today. Now, they have several cameras, editing suites and software packages; in the case of the most successful influencers, professional photographers and videographers are the ones producing behind the scenes. With the potential to earn enormous incomes, influencers have invested in the content-creation process and treat themselves like independent media companies.

However, in the beginning, when making profit was not part of their thought process, they bootstrapped. They were fast, reactive and sources of regular newness. Not constant, but publishing posts or videos once or twice a week was enough for bloggers and vloggers to be considered prolific. For online audiences, these messy, relatable ports of inspiration and storytelling were thrilling, mainly because, at this point, lifestyle publishing was still dominated by monthly print titles. While magazine brands often used their websites to dump press-release-informed editorial deemed too boring to print in their pages, bloggers and vloggers treated the internet like a public diary. They published chatty blogs of rambling sentences, stream-of-consciousness ideas and inconsequential stories which had heart. Their work was completely candid and there was a sense of vulnerability in their lack of professionalism. Every piece of content existed purely because they wanted to own a small part of the internet, and the majority of the video or blogging content formats they adhered to were almost shocking in their simplicity, particularly by comparison to today's standards.

Consider modern YouTube videos, in which Logan Paul does a jet-ski jump in a pool and actor Will Smith bungee jumps from a helicopter into the Grand Canyon. A squad of flawless lifestyle vloggers share their experience of a private island using footage filmed by drones and Elijah Daniel vlogs having his face tattooed with the word 'phag' by fellow YouTuber Tana Mongeau. These videos have high production gloss and are extreme, adrenaline-fuelled and controversial, created to get as much attention as quickly as possible.

However, in the noughties, early influencers were publishing hobbyists focused on sharing gentler narratives, not conscious empire builders. Susie Lau – arguably the godmother of fashion blogging, who launched her website Style Bubble in 2006 – says she started posting because she was bored and wanted to do something fun in her spare time. Meanwhile, Bryan Yambao – better known as Bryanboy after the website he created in 2004 – began his digital journey to share pictures with his family during a six-week trip to Russia. Even when he was featured in *The New York Post* a year later, he has admitted there was no masterplan – he was posting photos from parties when he was drunk. Having a blog was just for fun – which is exactly why Zoe Sugg started her website and YouTube channel too. Her first vlog in 2009 – entitled '60 things in my bedroom' – was literally a video of her holding sixty items she owned, one by one, to the soundtrack of then Myspace star Kate Nash.

Meanwhile, Tanya Burr's was a make-up tutorial showing viewers how to re-create the look of Serena van der Woodsen, the main character of noughties television show *Gossip Girl*. Dina Tokio documents visiting her granny in the Cornish town of Bude and KSI plays a video game.

The style in which influencers produced early work and the phenomenal engagement this generated were huge stumbling blocks for traditional publishers when it came to understanding their value. After all, by comparison they were – by anyone's standards – better. They were focused on precision, excellence and established rules of storytelling: the who, what, where and why. They had researched their subjects, produced narratives that had relevant hooks and constructed careful journalism with substance. Multiple sources, facts, figures, light and shade. They were operating under the umbrella of legacy-driven publishing houses – owners of trusted titles that had authority and the ability to illustrate stories with unforgettable imagery produced by professional photographers.

Bloggers and YouTubers are no threat, they thought. Their work is amateur – it will go away. Prue Lewington, former fashion editor of Australia's *Sunday Telegraph* turned brand consultant, says: 'Traditional media definitely thought the blogging phenomenon was a passing trend.' However, rather than disappear, these influencers seemed to pre-empt the direction in which publishing was heading, where constant interaction and continual publishing were key to survival and would become the norm. Personal legacy achieved through years of sharing stories would become as desired and valuable as brand legacy. Many traditional media companies are still coming to terms with the loose minute-to-minute publishing required of them by social platforms, while some of the most established influencers had started to master this, pre-Twitter.

Essentially, the brands they bootstrapped were and continue to be reflective of them and their personalities; rather than endless planning and having the best equipment, they simply started. In fact, one of the most asked questions of any YouTuber by their followers is: 'How do I start a YouTube channel?' They always, without fail, reply that you simply start. Don't overthink it. Don't believe there is a checklist of things you need to be a vlogger, just get going. Bloggers share a similar approach. Having grown an audience of millions, the speed and freedom that independent digital publishing offers to influencers is something vlogger and entrepreneur Patricia Bright continues to love about the internet today. She says: 'The beautiful thing about YouTube is you can have an idea, shoot it, edit it and upload it in one day.' Fellow YouTuber and author Louise Pentland agrees. 'It was such an open space and there was nothing stopping you.'

However, the one thing they don't add to their advice is that, after you start, you mustn't stop. Consistency of tone and regularity of publishing is key to building an audience. Take Naomi Davis, also known by her brand name Love Taza. Her blog began as Rockstar Diaries in 2007 and, through this, she documented her life as a 21-year-old dance student and wife living in New York City. This featured her husband, Josh, their dog, Kingsley, and a continuous stream of colourful but modest outfits. From the very beginning she shared everything on her blog: the fact that she was a Mormon, that she was the only undergraduate student at Juilliard who was married and that she regretted not pursuing a dance career in Europe. Pre-Instagram, every post was crammed full of pictures showcasing the life she and Josh were creating and, although the content was not necessarily beautiful, it communicated something much more exciting – energy, spontaneity and happy imperfection.

Meanwhile, when YouTuber Zoe Sugg started vlogging, she had no real agenda other than to share the make-up she was using and cheap things she had found at car boot sales. Her life was entirely achievable and, twice a week like clockwork, she uploaded videos from her bedroom. Similar to the teenage girls watching her, she had doubts, fears and was scared of change. She wasn't sure what to do after school and felt directionless. Unlike her peers from sixth form, she didn't go to university, opting to do an interior design apprenticeship instead. Her very bootstrapped brand message was basically, it's okay if you're not sure about everything. It's okay if you just want to sit in your room and put on make-up. Because it's fun, and it's okay to have fun. It might have been a simple brand message, but nobody else at that point was saying it. Although female-focused media brands now embrace narratives of anti-perfection having realized this relatability drives online engagement, at the time of Zoella gathering pace they were almost entirely focused on aspiration. It may seem bizarre, given how many brands and influencers have popped up in her likeness, but at the start of the influencer revolution, Zoe Sugg was entirely countercultural.

Admitting imperfection was a key part of early influencers' appeal and something the successful ones have never abandoned. As author, stylist and early lifestyle blogger Latonya Staubs, AKA Latonya Yvette, says: 'While I don't share most of my life, what I do share – and how I share it – is really how I am. It's how I approach motherhood and life as a person walking this earth. Mistakes and all.'

This was a new type of media and its transparency and spontaneity could not be replicated by people working within large media organizations due to their vastly different agendas. While the former held the keys to their own publishing castle and could do whatever they liked, whenever they wanted to, the latter had sales targets, layers of sign-off and a house style to adhere to.

Early influencers had no overarching plan, script or, at this point, sales pitch. Most YouTubers started channels simply because they wanted to be part of YouTube. Most bloggers started websites because they liked writing and taking pictures. Regardless of what platform they chose to bootstrap on, their common goal was communication and they kept going because they enjoyed interacting with their audiences. This dedication to delivering something small, genuine and imperfect became the springboard that would attract millions to their content and result in lucrative global brand partnerships.

2 Audience-centric content creation

These days, most media websites with aggressive growth targets are creating editorial based on data according to analytics tools. So if a news story about a certain celebrity did well yesterday, let's do another one today. Give people more and more of what they want to ensure large volumes of traffic. A good editor knows exactly who and what is catnip to their different audiences across Facebook, Twitter, Instagram and via newsletter.

However, as well as being early adopters of using analytics tools to grow their audiences, influencers also asked their followers questions – and crucially, they listened to their answers. In fact, the most successful ones are still highly invested in producing the content their followers and subscribers want to see. What do they want next – back-to-school make-up tutorials? Get ready with me vlogs? They are keen to understand their viewers' problems and be part of the solution.

Explaining how she accelerated growth on YouTube, Bright says: 'People wanted product reviews and lots of new brands were popping up. I continued to create content about that, and this is when I grew. When one thing works well, you just repeat it and repeat it. Older followers do get sick of it though, so it's a case of balancing what the old and new want.'

For Violet Gaynor, who co-founded parenting website The Glow in 2011, putting the brand on social media made her realize just how important that audience interaction was. She and her business partner Kelly Stuart had made the decision to disable the comments functionality of the site, as children were being featured and they believed this would make it feel like a safer space. However, follower feedback confirmed they were creating content that their target market actually desired and to which they had an emotional response. 'When we launched our social media, the interaction from followers showed us how much people wanted and needed what we were doing,' she says.

Herein lies an enormous difference between traditional digital media growth and influencer audience growth. The former is simply looking at uniques, dwell and bounce rates, often paying no attention to the feelings elicited by the content in question. Yes, those stories about that certain celebrity may be popular but it is entirely plausible that people are clicking through because they dislike the individual and want to leave critical comments. Due to this, many websites created by traditional media are toxic spaces driven by Twitter-style conflict.

Meanwhile, influencers have a much closer relationship with their audiences and, actually, large clickthrough for negative reasons is bad for business. The success of their websites, YouTube channels and social media relies on everyone getting along and acting like a group of friends, albeit with the influencer being top of the tree. When building their audiences initially, any sense that they were inauthentic or bitchy could kill their brand dead in the water. Trust and safety were paramount to getting things going, and therefore a two-way conversation between influencer and reader or viewer was the most efficient way to ensure their loyalty and adoration.

This is why many influencers can seem bland or out of touch with the real world, sharing very little in the way of opinions which might lead to controversy or disagreement. While some are simply not interested in current affairs, others have made a conscious decision to avoid them completely. For example, Bright admits she will never touch on politics. 'I'm not saying it's not important but my channels aren't the place where you're going to get that,' she says.

Meanwhile, Joe Sugg was clear when he started his YouTube channel in 2011 that he wouldn't cover any subject that was remotely controversial and this consistency has served him well. His followers are united by their love of him and therefore there is very little arguing in the comments below his videos or across social media. An adoring public is far easier for an influencer to manage – they can sell-out merchandise, have clarity in the style of content that works and offer a safe community to younger viewers or readers. This is especially important for YouTubers as many have a majority audience that is under eighteen years old.

Meanwhile, there are others for whom courting controversy is a key part of their brand. These people tend to have enormous audiences and have only started to truly utilize their ability to cause uproar after building huge, core fan bases.

Prime examples? Logan Paul and KSI. The pair – who are followed by millions on their respective channels and have branched out into film, music and sport – initially published controversial content unwittingly. It seemed they just didn't realize they were being tone deaf; given both individuals have grown up inside a YouTube celebrity bubble, this is completely plausible.

However, with controversy being a key part of both their brands, the pair teamed up in 2018 to exploit this fully via squaring up to each other in a globally hyped boxing match. Dubbed the 'biggest internet event ever', the first fight was judged as a draw while KSI emerged as the victor of their second in November 2019. Despite claiming to hate each other during the build-up to each fight, the truth is that their audiences engaged heavily with the YouTubers' conflict, which in turn meant conflict was good for business.

As Bright did with beauty product reviews in the early days of her YouTube channel, KSI and Paul will continue to deliver this narrative because it drives growth. Calgary Avansino – *Vogue* editor turned wellness influencer turned startup CEO – believes the supply and demand growth strategy of early influencers has become entirely expected by consumers. She says: 'People are now an integral part of the media they are consuming – modern media is not a lean-back experience.'

3   Understanding accumulative depth

Prior to the rise of influencers, there were editorial rules which defined storytelling. Content had to be rich in detail, succinct and without question have a clear beginning, middle and end. Stories were delivered neatly, with wit and intelligence. If you weren't clever, connected or deemed a brilliant writer, you weren't telling stories. Full stop.

However, this was another way in which influencers broke the system. Rather than applying for jobs at magazines and newspapers and asking permission to be storytellers, they decided that their story was one that must be told and they would do this independently. Also, it was a long-term project. The idea that your story could continue for years meant neat delivery was impossible. Blogs and vlogs were just the latest instalments of ongoing narratives, more like soap operas than journalism or traditional writing. The point was to keep going no matter what – even if your week had been boring or you have nothing much to say, you must say something. Their stories live in a liminal space and part of their appeal is that they are never finished.

For Purvis, this ongoing documentation was easy to maintain as it was the only aspect of her life to which she felt completely connected. She says: 'Between dropping out of university and interning, it was the one constant thing I had and felt passionate about.'

This rule-breaking is another thing that perplexes anyone unfamiliar with the world of influencers, who is used to features packed with information, interviews and facts reflecting the zeitgeist. Why do people want to read or watch this stuff? Viewed in isolation, a singular influencer post or video can seem, at best, navel-gazing and, at worst, boring.

However, influencers understood yet another key element of digital media ahead of anyone else – the power of accumulative depth.

At this point, you might argue: 'But what about columnists?' They've been drip-feeding segments of long-term stories for ages. But remember the new rules created by influencers:

a No neatness.

b No clear or succinct beginning, middle and end.

c They are the most prevalent subject.

Influencers are staggering information and accumulating depth across multiple platforms every day. Some of that depth is intended and well thought out in the form of vlogs and blogs, but other parts of it are more ephemeral. Spontaneous tweets. Drunken Instagram Stories with friends. It all adds up to something that feels like a true and authentic window into an individual's life, and the influencer builds upon this every single day. In comparison, a weekly column feels somewhat thin – even if the writer is a master tweeter too.

The influencers most invested in accumulative depth are the daily vloggers, who are documenting their lives every single day regardless of what happens. A prime example of accumulation leading to enormous success is YouTube channel SacconeJolys, which documents the lives of a family of six living in Surrey headed up by Irish parents Anna and Jonathan. Their brand strap-line? 'Life is about the little things.' And so, their millions of followers accompany them to soft play, on date nights and to the hairdresser. However, they have also witnessed enormous events in the couple's lives including the births of their four children, their wedding day and them buying a home. They've seen their children take their first steps, listened – and supported – Anna through her experience of postnatal depression, and cheered on the family as they've gone from emergent YouTubers to international brand. When Anna miscarried at eleven weeks in 2016, the outpouring of grief online was extraordinary and, with it, many of the family's viewers shared their own devastation about past miscarriages.

This accumulation of depth means subscribers to the SacconeJolys are truly invested in their story. It's not something they can take or leave, it's a narrative they have been following and interacting with since 2009. So, while they are there for the big milestones, memories and tragedies, they will also tune in to watch Jonathan playing tag with the children in the garden. The audience relishes each and every update.

However, it is not just the daily vloggers who benefit from the power of accumulative depth. Thanks to the possibility of easy daily publishing across social media, less frequent vloggers – who perhaps post a weekly update – also draw a huge crowd of people keen to learn about the nitty-gritty of their past seven days.

Cleverly, this kind of influencer turns their content drop into an event that their followers simply can't miss. A master of this is lifestyle YouTuber Lydia Millen, who publishes weekly vlogs on Sunday nights, encouraging followers across social media to 'settle down with a cup of tea'. These videos can be up to an hour long – in comparison to the average twenty minutes of the daily vlogger – and, in truth, destroy the notion that millennials have no attention span.

Meanwhile, there is also the Michalaks – a family of four, led by parents Hannah and Stefan, who are explicitly trying to create weekly vlogs more akin to television than YouTube. They have a very specific aesthetic, combining humorous voiceovers with traditional vlogging and comedic skits. The thing that sets them apart in the weekly YouTube content drop? Production. Their professional approach to sound and editing means their subscribers return as much for the update as they do for the high quality of their entertainment.

And what about the bloggers? As attention moves ever more towards visuals, live broadcasting and video, many have abandoned their websites as a way of perpetuating accumulative depth in favour of social media. Instagram has become a place for pictures accompanied by long captions – essentially, a place to blog – while Stories is a way to share video content without having to build an audience on YouTube. Blogs – the place where many influencers started to accumulate depth with their audiences – are largely turning into spaces populated by poorly written sponsored content. As being an influencer has become viable as a full-time career, their motivation has changed from communication to money-making and the quick money is on Instagram.

Only people – influencers, essentially – can adopt an accumulative depth strategy, as it relies upon personality, charisma and overcoming struggle. Subscribers and followers continue to consume content based on the simple fact they care about the person or people creating it, not because they are necessarily hugely compelled by the information being shared.

4   Confessional moments

With so much of influencer content being driven by consumerism – product edits, things they like, home tours and hauls – a key route to maintaining intimacy with audiences is confessional moments. Through this, the influencer draws their followers into their confidence – regardless of the fact that they are doing this in a public way with an enormous number of people. It also reinforces the sense that, just like their followers, they are human beings with struggles to overcome, something that is important to push given their lives become more fantastical as they gain success.

Consider this: an influencer's initial, core audience was probably drawn to them because they were relatable but perhaps presenting their life in a slightly more beautiful or humorous way. As brand partnerships become a focus, communities can start to turn on the influencers – criticizing them for their commercial content and lamenting over the early days when they weren't trying to sell them anything. YouTuber Jana Hisham, who started her channel in 2010, highlights: 'You simply can't be a relatable character if you're now living a life of luxury which doesn't involve much adversity or personal development.' Influencers reminding their followers that they are human is imperative for this relationship to continue – and ironically, for their followers to buy in to the products they promote. It's all connected.

In their confessional moments, influencers will often share experiences that impacted on them as children – for example, dealing with bullies or recovering from an eating disorder. However, it would be inaccurate to say that deeply personal content is entirely a cynical ploy to maintain popularity. One should never underestimate how influencers have destroyed taboos and created spaces for their followers to talk about critical issues such as loneliness, depression and anxiety since the social media revolution began and early influencers trail-blazed this open approach.

For example, YouTuber Nathan Zed turned his own battle with feelings of worthlessness into a product line after a video he created, 'You're not good enough', drove serious conversation about self-belief. His followers' admissions that they felt under pressure to be perfect or conform to an ideal led him to create his first collection of hoodies and t-shirts. These were printed with the slogan 'Good Enough' and swiftly sold out in 2017. He dropped a further two collections in 2018, one of which was accompanied by a series of Spotify playlists about mental health.

Meanwhile, one of the most impactful kinds of announcement made by YouTubers is their coming out stories. These videos are often the first time they talk about this with their audiences and tend to include how they feel about their sexuality, their realization they were gay, bi- or pansexual and how they told their parents.

Scott Major, founder of gaming YouTube channel DangThatsALongName, had been out for a few years in real life before announcing it online in 2018. He says: 'I realized I owed it to my audience – and to all the people out there who were struggling with their sexual identity – to use my platform and reach to help them realize that being LGBT+ wasn't something to be ashamed or scared of.'

'I was a young, happy, successful gay man, which wasn't something I'd seen a lot of growing up, and I wanted to show people that my sexuality didn't have to define me, but it was still a big part of who I am.'

Following his coming-out video, he received an influx of emails and tweets from his followers expressing their support and revealing how Scott's honesty had helped them talk about their own sexuality. He says: 'If I was able to make even just one person be more comfortable with who they are, I had done my job.'

However, not every confessional moment is a big announcement. There are more low-key videos and posts from influencers sharing the fact that on that day they have struggled with parenthood or their career. Meanwhile, others will take a long-term approach to this by posting continual updates on a highly personal issue. Sobriety, for example, has become a growing area for influencer discussion. Blogger and YouTuber David Gibbs, partner of fellow vlogger Ebony Day, has covered his journey from alcoholism to fatherhood on his website Lessons In Being Alive. This includes his belief in God and his battle with depression in the context of how he sees life since having had a daughter. In addition to longer updates on his blog, he also shares sobriety milestones on Twitter and Instagram.

Journalist, columnist, campaigner and social media star Bryony Gordon documents her journey from addiction to sobriety across a national newspaper (*The Telegraph*), Instagram and Twitter. She has posted content about her realization that she was an addict, her experience of rehab and the steps she has taken to recover, which include self-acceptance and daily exercise with a focus on calming her mind rather than shrinking her body.

At the other end of the spectrum, there are confessional break-up videos – necessary for many influencers as they often end up in relationships with each other and therefore it is immediately obvious when they stop spending time together. When questions and comments from their audiences reach fever pitch, they release a video or post detailing why their relationship ended to halt speculation. Influencer break-ups that have caused huge ripples and led to confessional videos or essays have been those of Ben Brown and Nicole Eddy, Will Darbyshire and Alexa Losey, and Emily Canham and Jake Boys. Bucking the trend are early YouTubing husband and wife Tanya Burr and Jim Chapman, who announced their 2019 split on Instagram Stories and made it clear any further details about the end of their relationship were strictly off limits.

Whatever the subject of an influencer's confessional moment, the format is always the same: either a long, almost stream-of-consciousness blog or a to-camera monologue telling their story and answering questions. Interestingly, when it is in the latter format and it is coming from a lifestyle influencer, many still share links within the video as to what they are wearing at the time. They might be approaching a sensitive subject, but it's still a case of business as usual.

5 Rebrand, rebrand, rebrand

Many influencers who started publishing in approximately 2007 chose handles, blog titles and channel names that were either super feminine or reflective of the timing, referencing gaming or pop culture. As time went on and their audiences grew, these influencers felt those original names – which had now come to represent their brand – no longer seemed appropriate. So what did they do? They rebranded.

Rebranding is a key strength of the influencer and part of the reason their content can feel so timely and nimble. For many, this means new handles across social media, a new website with new fonts and graphic design, and perhaps a new focus. Since 2015, influencers who launched their platforms with a tight focus on fashion or beauty have moved towards working under the umbrella term of 'lifestyle', meaning they also cover interiors, travel, food and – if it's relevant to them – marriage, pregnancy and parenting. This allows them to comfortably share a more thorough view of their lives and be candidates for a greater number of brand partnerships.

Meanwhile, gamers who started out by sharing videos of themselves playing FIFA have graduated to playing the latest releases (most likely zeitgeist games such as Apex Legends, Fortnite: Battle Royale, and shooter games such as Battlefield, Call of Duty, Destiny and League of Legends). They have also added the live-streaming platform Twitch to their offering and share edits of their streams on YouTube, alongside gaming commentary.

Following a major rebrand, an influencer will often explain that they no longer felt comfortable with the style of content they were producing or believed it was time to freshen up their platforms. For those working in the lifestyle arena, this often means ditching a moniker they believed to be cool when they were a teenager and making their brand eponymous. Amber Fillerup was previously Barefoot Blonde, Patricia Bright was BritPop Princess and Alfie Deyes was Pointless Blog. Other influencers rebranded from names that suggested a very specific type of content to something that could encompass a broader output. Anna Newton's Vivianna Does Makeup became The Anna Edit, while Lynsey Neil's Miss West End Girl became Lynsey Loves. Even Zoe Sugg has separated herself from Zoella. This now refers to her business ventures while anything directly personal to her is eponymous.

When it comes to influencer rebrands, the point is to revamp their platforms and align their content with where their life is. Take aforementioned blogger Naomi Davis. She began her blog as Rockstar Diaries, detailing life as a young newlywed and sharing her eclectic styling alongside products she liked. However, when she started having children, her focus changed. Fashion took a backseat to parenting, nursery design and raising children in New York City. At that point, her platforms became branded as Love Taza.

Similarly, Esther Coren closed the food blog she had started in 2007 to launch a general lifestyle website, The Spike, in 2014. She says: 'It came to a natural conclusion when I had just clean run out of things to cook and was also bored with talking about food.'

Influencers have no fear of change, particularly early adopters of YouTube who have often pivoted several times, starting and closing channels if they lose interest or want to try something new.

Comedic political vlogger Taha Khan says: 'My first YouTube channel was a dance one, then I did a gaming one. I started wanting to do comedy in 2013 because I thought it looked like fun.'

Meanwhile, Major says he would start channels and stop them if they were failing to engage people. When he launched DangThatsALongName he intended to focus on producing skit and vlogging content, but soon refocused to gaming and Minecraft. 'That was what my true passion was,' he says.

Influencer rebrands can be gradual and subtle following milestones such as leaving university, marriage and giving birth or more dramatic, including new brand names, websites and logos. The fact is, early-moving influencers have managed to hold their audiences' attention for over a decade because they move with the tide. As they are changing, so too do their platforms. Unlike regular brands, theirs is never truly static but always evolving.

6 Establishing ecosystems

When working out how influencers created these colossal followings devoted to their independent, bootstrapped brands, it's worth remembering this: they did not do it alone. In the early days of YouTube, there was a relatively small group of content creators and they all formed loose partnerships. They hosted informal meet-ups for their viewers and fellow YouTubers, created videos together and even moved to the same part of the world. Outside of New York and Los Angeles, the YouTuber capital of the world is arguably Brighton in the UK – home to PewDiePie, Zoe Sugg and Alfie Deyes, to mention just three. They commented on each other's videos and started friendships in real life. After all, they were doing something independently which – at that time – very few people valued or understood. It made sense to get to know and collaborate with others who did. As YouTuber Hisham notes: 'The most successful collaborations emerged from real-life friends.'

Something similar happened in the world of blogging as bloggers would meet at events, be seated together and over time became friends. Lucy Nicholls recalls how ecosystems would start through chance meetings in real life and then develop into exciting projects. She became friends with fellow early influencer Carrie Santana da Silva – founder of blog Wish Wish Wish – when they were on the same university course. 'I very much admired her, she was at the forefront of blogging and carried me along with her,' she says. 'She told me to photograph myself and make my photos bigger.'

Thanks to attending press days together, she and Santana da Silva ended up becoming friends with fellow bloggers Purvis and Kristabel Plummer, and together they founded shopping event The Bloggers' Market, through which they sold clothes and hosted creative workshops. The group continue to make content together, although Nicholls is the only one who chose not to be a full-time influencer. 'I don't regret it,' she says. 'I never thought my proposition was strong enough to sustain a career and there were other things I wanted to explore.'

Between 2013 and 2015, the same thing happened on Instagram. Buoyed by the then digital trend of #squadgoals – content that featured groups of influencers who were all friends – ecosystems popped up and, through the cross-promotion of each others' accounts, their audiences grew at an enviable rate. They discovered that two people – or a group of people – having fun was more compelling than one. It also added another level of appeal to each individual influencer – not only did they have an interesting life at home but they also travelled the world and hung out with equally compelling friends. While squad goals is a 'nice to have' for lifestyle influencers, it is almost a necessity for gamers and entertainment vloggers due to the fact so many games are of online multi-player in format, and so many challenge trend video formats – a staple for this kind of YouTuber – require several people.

Take Sidemen – a team of gamers with a dedicated YouTube channel, made up of KSI, Vik Barn, Simon Minter, Harry Lewis, Tobi Brown, Joshua Bradley and Ethan Payne. They have lived together at various points, stream their gaming progress on Twitch, and take on challenges once a week.

Then there is Jack Mason, AKA JackFrags, who games with his old friends, Two Angry Gamers. However the ultimate squad goals in terms of gaming happened in March 2018 when Drake, Travis Scott and Juju played Fortnite on Twitch with professional player Tyler Blevins, AKA Ninja. The appeal of multiplayer gaming streams is the commentary and conversation between the different gamers. It is useful, funny and relatable, reflecting the real-life experience of viewers.

The downside of ecosystems? It's worth noting that a squad of five people with one million followers each does not equal a combined audience of five million. There is so much cross-pollination and promotion between influencers, that the reality is many of those people will follow or subscribe to every account in the ecosystem. However, when putting together press trips or curating influencer guest lists for events, understanding ecosystems is imperative. If judged correctly, you will have a group of people who understand how to make content together and who their audiences already believe to be friends.

HOW A CHANCE MEETING LED TO AN ECOSYSTEM

IT WAS 2015 AND IN London the most fashionable thing you could do as a new mum was attend networking events organized by Mothers Meeting. A key offering of the business – founded by graphic designer Jenny Scott – were these sessions and panels aimed at women who were just as passionate about their careers as they were about having children.

The interesting thing about the strongest influencer ecosystems is so many began by chance through bloggers and vloggers becoming friends in real life first. And, by chance, Clemmie Hooper, Clemmie Telford, Steph Douglas and Zoe de Pass – later four of the UK's most prominent parenting influencers – met at a Mothers Meeting event before any of them had accumulated the Instagram followings for which they are famous today.

Together, they represented a very modern kind of motherhood which involved retaining their pre-baby identity and admitting parenting was not a picture-perfect experience. Cheerful, but not perfect. Telford says: 'It was a real zeitgeist moment and most of us were sharing stuff on Instagram already, mostly for our own sanity.' She adds: 'We genuinely became friends because we were able to say that although we loved having kids and a career, it was hard.'

Discussing work has remained a key part of their narratives online, and this began at Mothers Meeting. 'It was all about owning the fact you were an ambitious woman who happened to have a baby strapped to her chest,' says Telford. 'It is so important that women are able to talk about their careers.'

For Hooper, Mothers Meeting was a relief. She says: 'I just thought "finally – people who are interested in us as women not just as mothers".' In the years that have followed, the group, along with fellow influencers Anna Whitehouse (AKA Mother Pukka) and Natalie Lee, have worked on campaigns together, attended festivals and generally featured in each other's content as a result of becoming good friends. However, there was a tabloid backlash instigated by Mumsnet message boards, criticizing the lifestyle of the group and how they made money in 2017. At this point they were branded 'Insta-mums' by the *Daily Mail*.

Hooper says: 'Our friendship goes much deeper than Instagram. Our husbands all get along and we chat on WhatsApp nearly everyday. It's weird, people just don't trust a group of women.'

THE SUCCESS OF FIVE EARLY ADOPTING BLOGGERS

Huda Kattan: when Kattan left her finance job in Dubai to relocate to Los Angeles, re-train as a make-up artist and start a beauty blog in 2008, her parents were disappointed. As Iraqi immigrants who had brought her up in America, they had hoped she would pursue medicine or law. However, this led to her product line – Huda Beauty, launched in 2013 – which retails make-up, fragrance and lashes, and was valued at over £1bn by Forbes in 2018. Her products have been praised for their inclusivity of skin tone, which she believes is a key element in why the business is so successful.

Emily Weiss: thanks to a day job at US *Vogue*, Weiss's blog – Into The Gloss – quickly became a must-read after launching in 2010. Not only did she have access to a plethora of high-profile interviewees, she also understood the importance of attention to detail and brand. These three key elements established her influence and elevated her website, which she would work on at 5 am before heading to the office. In 2014, she launched her skincare and beauty brand, Glossier, and in 2019, a colour-focused make-up sister line, Glossier Play. The same year as the latter release, the company was valued at $1.2bn.

Leandra Medine: three days after New Yorker Medine launched her fashion blog, Man Repeller, in 2010, it was featured by digital lifestyle publishing juggernaut Refinery29. Why? The concept behind its existence: it was dedicated to trends that women love, but men couldn't bear. Now a fully fledged media brand in its own right, Man Repeller has an editorial team, frequently works on campaigns with fashion brands and in 2016 launched shoe brand MR by Man Repeller.

Margaret Zhang: just sixteen years old in 2009 when she started her blog, Shine By Three, Sydney native Zhang's initial motivation was her love of fashion. However, these days she is a prolific stylist and creative director for publications such as *Marie Claire* and *Harper's Bazaar*, not to mention a consultant for brands including Louis Vuitton and Uniqlo. She has also starred in global campaigns and is particularly sought after for her wisdom in digital marketing.

Tavi Gevinson: when Gevinson started her blog Style Rookie at just eleven years of age, it was a series of posts featuring her wearing quirky outfits with commentary on trends. Her work was soon noticed and featured by *The New York Times*, and following this she made headlines by attending Paris and New York Fashion Weeks. In 2011, she launched fashion and feminism website Rookie and published four yearbooks, featuring its best content. Although the brand folded in 2018, Gevinson has moved into theatre and film, working as an actor and taking occasional commissions as a freelance writer.

KEY TAKEAWAYS

- The most prominent influencers today were early adopters of social media and blogging and entered the digital space at a time when it was much less congested. However, being ahead of the curve isn't the only reason they have managed to maintain their popularity. Due to years spent consistently sharing their life stories, they have a significant legacy and many of their followers may have been following their story for a decade or more.
- Early influencers were counterculture to traditional media in a way that their audience enjoyed due to their relatable narratives. Unlike lifestyle publications at the time, which were focused on aspiration, they wore affordable clothes and spoke about their imperfections. In short, they were extremely human and understood the power of regular publishing.
- They cared not just about the number of views and visits their work accumulated but the human reaction to it in the comments sections of their blogs and YouTube channels. They also created a supply and demand pattern, by asking their followers what content they wanted. This deeply audience-centric system of content creation allowed influencers to learn more about their followers' problems and then become part of the solution.

- Influencer content should not be viewed as singular pieces in isolation but as an extensive body of work that has been developed over a significant period of time. The resulting depth of what they have produced is part of their value.
- Rebranding their platforms to ensure these represent their particular stage of life or to signal a change in direction is a key influencer strength. They are not scared of change, and as they are documenting their own lives – and many started their platforms as teenagers – it would lack authenticity if they stayed the same.
- Many of the early influencers grew their audiences through creating digital ecosystems which were the result of becoming friends in real life. Through appearing in each other's content and cross-promotions they were able to gain greater visibility quickly. However, it is worth noting that this means there is most likely a large audience crossover within any one ecosystem.

3

The business of influence: monetizing the industry

Early-adopting influencers had built audiences and were moving towards constructing a new kind of entertainment landscape dominated by video, blogs and constant interaction with their readers and viewers. However, until approximately 2012, creating content for their websites and social media, by and large, remained a hobby. Those for whom it did generate income admit any earnings simply supplemented another, more traditional career. Lifestyle vlogger and author Louise Pentland started her blog in 2009 and her YouTube channel in 2010 but 'didn't see a penny' until 2012. 'I was working as a receptionist part-time and thought if I could make £500 a month from that and blogging I would be okay,' she says. The idea one could negotiate a five-figure campaign deal at this point was ludicrous. Pentland says: 'Making money wasn't the goal, everything was about making content that people loved.' Fellow YouTuber, blogger, author and entrepreneur Patricia Bright agrees. 'It just wasn't monetizable back then and there wasn't a strategy to turn it into a business.'

While the early influencers were not driven by money enough to convert their popularity into pay cheques, there were people observing their rise and what this could potentially mean for brands. These individuals became the first wave of influencer managers – a resilient bunch of rough-and-ready opportunists, keen to turn extraordinary video views and subscriber numbers into the linchpins of persuasive pitches for sponsorship deals. They saw influencers' stories as commodities they could leverage based on the fact there was such evident demand for them and were more akin to salespeople than talent managers. In fact, these early industry-makers still hold this position and aggressively protect the worth of what their clients are selling. One influencer manager – whose roster features the world's most popular YouTubers – refused access to his talent for this book, based on the fact they would not financially benefit from sharing information about their journey in this way, but the publishing house would. No money, no story. The idea they would freely give away any insight into their lives for zero financial reward was, to him, not just implausible but, frankly, bad for business.

The second generation of managers came from existing talent-focused companies or were people already working in media, who saw launching influencer divisions or acquiring influencer marketing agencies as a way of not being left behind by this emergent, desired market. Already experienced in putting together traditional advertising campaigns that featured talent, they were from the worlds of marketing, advertising, modelling and celebrity, and treated the formula for producing influencer creative as they would any other. This added an arguably much-needed sheen of professionalism to the space but didn't necessarily result in the most compelling work. The influencers were accustomed to creative freedom and their content-creation process was often reactionary. Their power lay in their human approach – the natural rhythm of their speech, their flaws and their honesty. Yet with the second wave of industry monetization came scripts, strict guidelines and – in some cases – inauthentic brand deals.

Speaking of brands, they were getting wiser and wiser about the power of influencer marketing and experiencing first-hand the fact successful partnerships could drive traffic, audience numbers and sales. They were also becoming keenly aware of cultural relevancy and how, in a wider media landscape where everyone was represented, they had to diversify to stay current. Influencer partnerships were allowing them to tap into new demographics and reposition themselves by proxy.

Then came the platforms. As it became clear that targeting the right people with content they were statistically likely to engage with was crucial, searchable data-scraping systems which quantified influencers via growth rates and audience demographics sprang up. Meanwhile, another set of tech and marketing entrepreneurs identified the problem with influencer marketing to be a difficulty connecting brands and influencers. Their solution? Online marketplaces, where brands could commission and sign off cheap and cheerful content, which influencers would post on their platforms with pre-agreed messaging.

Due to lack of standardization, the monetization of digital influence and value attributed to content creators remains the major sticking point for those attempting to capitalize on it. A much uttered statement is that it's like the 'wild west' and, indeed, there seems to be little logic behind influencer fees. Meanwhile, on the other side of the table, some brands are willing to throw enormous sums of money at these campaigns to experience the influx of digital popularity their association stands to deliver, whatever the cost.

The first wave of influencer capitalists

Before Liam Chivers started his influencer agency OP Talent in 2012 – and became the manager of YouTube behemoths KSI and Ali-A to name just two major names on his books – he was a sales trader working for a video games manufacturer. 'We made six million discs a day and I had good contacts in gaming,' he says.

YouTube became visible on his radar after he and his wife had their first child. Having met couples who also had children at the same time through

British prenatal support organization NCT, he and his new dad friends started gaming together on Friday nights. He says: 'I would watch YouTube to get better and get tips. At that point, we were playing Call of Duty (COD) and I wasn't a fan of YouTubers but did find myself watching the same people over and over again.'

As luck would have it, he had a meeting with Activision – the publisher of COD – in June 2012 at one of the industry's biggest conventions, E3. He flew to Los Angeles for the event and, while doing the rounds, he noticed someone familiar.

'I saw this scruffy young lad walking across the hall and recognized this was a guy I had been watching called xJawz. I looked at his badge and he had managed to get in with a fake pass to get industry information on COD,' he says.

xJawz was one of YouTube's first gaming influencers and known offline as Sam Betesh. He had started his channel when he was fifteen years old and had a strategy of publishing two or three videos a day through which he would share information on how to play COD and win.

Betesh immediately clocked Chivers' iPhone case – it featured the video game he was obsessed with and had been given to Chivers as a present during his meeting with Activision. Long story short, Chivers gave him the case and Betesh said he would tweet him as a thank you from his popular Twitter account. 'It was worth $2, but to a gamer it was a collectors' item,' says Chivers.

Over the next few hours, he watched in amazement as he accumulated hundreds of new Twitter followers due to Betesh's one tweet. He could see the power of digital influencers was real but wasn't quite sure of how he fitted into the picture until he was at his second major industry conference that year: Gamescom. He had given gaming YouTuber Alastair Aiken – AKA Ali-A – passes to the event and introduced him to his contacts at Activision. As a result, he spent three days on the company's stand playing COD. Aiken's reaction to this experience made it clear to Chivers what his next step was. He says: 'Ali looked me in the eye and said, "This is incredible – I need an agent".'

Having seen the IT disc industry destroyed by the CD, Chivers knew his days selling discs were inevitably numbered. 'I wanted to be there at the start of the revolution,' he says. 'I spent the next couple of weeks getting in touch with every business I knew to start pitching.' As a result, energy drinks brand Monster became Aiken's sponsor. This partnership lasted for six years.

Chivers' high-enthusiasm, low-strategy approach to monetizing Ali-A's content was that of an opportunistic salesperson – he saw possibility and moved quickly. This wasn't talent management in the traditional sense, as to broker that first deal he was focused on discovering interested parties with a budget and appetite for YouTube promotion, rather than strategically plotting the gamer's ascent. However, like a human sledgehammer, Chivers was breaking ground to start building an industry. This is something Simon Chambers, owner of Storm Management, who started working with influencers in 2014, applauds him for. 'To make a market, you need someone to do that at a point where nobody understands the potential of what is possible or what the opportunities are.'

Chivers speedily established himself almost at the same time as the initial brand desire to work with gaming YouTubers was happening. He registered his management agency OP Talent to Companies House on September 24th, 2012, signed Olajide Olatunji – AKA KSI – and Ali-A within two months of each other, and continues to represent both. To give a sense of how their careers have developed under his watch, in a 2014 poll by US trade publication *Variety*, KSI was voted more influential to American teenagers than any traditional celebrity.[1] In addition, a 2018 boxing match between him and fellow YouTuber Logan Paul generated revenue of $11 million, according to *Business Insider*. The 2019 follow-up fight resulted in both getting a reported payout of $900K. Meanwhile, Ali-A was the most watched gaming influencer on YouTube in 2018. Despite having no hesitancy to build a company in the then unestablished world of influencer marketing, Chivers admits he did not foresee this level of success. He says: 'I didn't know how big it would be. At the start it was such a battle and it still is some days, but it has become much more appreciated.'

Like all early-adopting YouTubers, his clients began publishing videos because they loved the platform and communicating with their audiences. Now, however, it's business. He says: 'They are focused on success and continue to do well because they are fast, consistent, produce relatable content and interact with their audiences. These guys are tweeting them and answering their comments – it's completely and utterly down to engagement.' Endemol Shine UK acquired OP Talent in 2016.

While Chivers was arguably the first person to recognize the potential to build a market around gaming influencers, he wasn't the first person to trailblaze monetization of YouTube's lifestyle space. This was Dominic Smales, who founded digital talent agency Gleam Futures. Like Chivers, he had a career in sales and marketing before moving into digital. A health scare which resulted in a six-month break to recover made him reconsider what he wanted to do and he realized his passion was social media. In a 2018 interview with beauty journalist Emma Gunavardhana for her podcast – The Emma Guns Show – he said: 'It was in the days when Facebook was blowing up and YouTube was starting to get traction.'[2]

His business began as a social media consultancy in 2010 called Gleam Digital and Smales worked regularly with Chanel, advising the brand on how it could connect with online audiences. The catalyst for his move into the influencer space? Watching sisters Samantha and Nicola Chapman on their beauty-focused YouTube channel Pixiwoo.

He told Gunavardhana: 'I was absolutely fascinated by the fact these two girls were popping up on the homepage of YouTube pretty much every week, and driving more engagement, comments and views than a lot of the viral videos that were generally the content you'd find on YouTube in those days.'

The passionate response they elicited from their subscribers was the first step towards Smales' eureka moment which turned consultancy Gleam Digital into talent agency Gleam Futures. 'The phenomenon was that audiences were watching these guys not just for the learning, but because they were into them and their lives and personalities,' he said.

Working from a coffee shop near his home, he began giving the sisters commercial advice. They later introduced him to fellow YouTubers Tanya Burr, their brother Jim Chapman and Ruth Crilly. 'It was like we were building a family business,' he told Gunavardhana.

Smales admitted he was uncertain about which direction the influencer industry would go in but he had no doubts about its potential to boom. 'The only thing I knew for sure was this was definitely going to grow.'

Gleam has since become synonymous with some of the world's most successful YouTubers (the company calls its talent 'digital first'). Although it lost three major names in 2017 – Caspar Lee, Joe Sugg and Alfie Deyes – it continues to represent noted vloggers including those initial clients who helped Smales build his business as well as numerous content creators with mass audiences, including Zoe Sugg.

Like Chivers, he revealed the ongoing success of his clients is down to their attitude. In the interview with Gunavardhana, he said: 'It's never not about hard work and focus.'

Gleam received significant investment of an undisclosed amount from agency group Dentsu Aegis in 2017.

The industry in its second era

If the first generation of managers broke ground to establish the market, the second wave moved soon after to grab a share of brand marketing budgets, which, by 2014, were being split out to include dedicated influencer spend. Someone who spotted the growing tide of interest was the aforementioned Simon Chambers, who set up a dedicated department for digital talent at Storm – the global modelling agency he owns – the same year.

'I can't decide if it was defensive or offensive, but it was clear the space was taking off in a big way,' he says. 'Brands were working more and more with

YouTubers and bloggers and we could see it was becoming an exciting place.' To comprehend this new generation of talent better, Chambers headed to YouTube conference VidCon that year. 'I didn't understand anything anyone was saying,' he recalls. 'I was the oldest person there and made hundreds of notes. I went back for three years to build up my knowledge.' Doing this gave Chambers an edge on his competition, as many agencies were also adapting to sign digital talent, but he realized early on – thanks to VidCon – that YouTube was 'a world of its own'. Although he made the move to include influencers on his books with a focus on the video platform, he believes the Instagram influencer explosion has blurred the lines which previously separated the people he represents. It is much easier to create content for Instagram, he says, and due to this there is now the sense anyone can be – and should be – an influencer. Speaking of how this broadening of the market has impacted on the talent Storm was founded for – models – he says: 'Every major contract states they'd like the model to post on social media as well. Everything has converged and approximated but we still see the difference between someone who has a large social following and whose primary career is something else, and content creators.'

Chambers can also fall back on the fact Storm has an established process when it comes to managing talent and brokering deals, which insulates him somewhat from the 'wild west' feeling of the industry that seems to make establishing trust between influencer agents and brands difficult.

Si Barbour-Brown, founder and director of digital talent agency The Sharper Group, believes brand suspicion is down to the profits-focused first era of the industry, when certain influencer managers were charging a premium and under-delivering. 'Some creators' management have set a bad example and continue to set a bad example but we're getting to a stage where people know who is and isn't professional,' he says. 'The fact is, this needn't be complicated and you shouldn't always have to pay five figures for a YouTube video.'

He also believes the approach of first-generation influencer management has been to the detriment of the influencers themselves. In his view, it is 'unbelievable' how few UK YouTubers have crossed over to television given how prominent they are globally and how long they have been in the public eye. He cites Joe Sugg as the 'only' person who has done really well thanks to his (almost) star turn on BBC One competition *Strictly Come Dancing* in 2018. 'He gave a really good account of himself and it has been great for YouTube,' he says.

Influencer technology: information meets connectivity

Influencer identification, quantifying their social data into demographics and connecting with them alongside managing and judging campaign success have been the main functions of numerous marketplace platforms developed during the first era of the influencer industry. A key piece of kit in the brand and agency toolbox, these have allowed marketers to advertise what they need for upcoming campaigns and influencers, in turn, can pitch for the work. These are useful as they allow users to quickly get in touch with a large pool of content creators who are keen to work on sponsored creative, find out key metrics about their audiences and manage the delivery of assets. They are problematic as they facilitate what is essentially a content churn – high volumes of work for many campaigns with influencers who will partner with a competitor the following day. Essentially, marketplaces give brands access to guns for hire. These are potentially effective for mass-targeted fast-moving consumer goods (FMCG) brands that want to create noise, but unlikely to work for those in the luxury or niche markets.

Most notable in this space is TRIBE, founded by former television and radio presenter Jules Lund who pioneered the influencer marketplace model when he launched his platform in 2015. In 2019, the company raised $7.5m in a Series A round of investment to break America, having successfully grown customer bases across Australia and the UK.

A challenger in the space is Influencer, founded by Ben Jeffries. His eureka moment for the platform came when he was fifteen years old and, as a young entrepreneur, working with Chelsea Football Club's reserve team to promote his clothing startup, Breeze. Although the content they created performed well, the players were hard to get in touch with and unsure of how to price themselves. And so Influencer was launched in 2015 offering brands data insights, creator discovery tools, relationship and campaign management software as well as campaign reporting capability. Jeffries' co-founder and chief marketing officer? Early-adopting YouTuber Caspar Lee.

The impact of brand desire for influencers

The catalyst for both eras of influencer management, not to mention the platform explosion? Brand deals and the potential to make significant profit, particularly from those still getting to grips with digital publishing and dealing with a daily feeling they were falling behind quick-moving competitors and fast-paced startups. As a result, desired influencers have been quickly elevated and become an integral part of brand communications.

In Australia, Prue Lewington – *Sunday Telegraph* fashion editor turned brand consultant – revealed those with audiences in the six-digits arena are treated like 'VIPs with celebrity status'. She says: 'They attend high-profile red-carpet events, sit front row at fashion week and are co-designing collections.' Instagram activity is most desired by brands and their PR shift has relegated traditional media due to the fact influencers will share news and events without a 'sensational' headline. Lewington says influencers now get 'first looks' at designers' latest collections and are fed breaking stories ahead of journalists.

It is a similar story in the United Arab Emirates, although there is a much more established tradition of inspiration coming from influencers in the region. Louise Nichol, who was editor-in-chief of *Harper's Bazaar Arabia* until

2018, describes them as being an 'incredibly important' part of the media landscape, and are in some cases placed on a 'higher rung' on which they can command a larger budget. She says: 'Even pre-digital influencers, the women who served as style icons – there is no Kate Moss equivalent in the country – were "real" women: socialites or entrepreneurs or creatives. So taking style cues from non-conventional celebrities is firmly rooted in the country.'

Brand desire for influencers to associate with their products is also down to the simple fact it has a positive impact on digital engagement, growth and sales, particularly in the fashion industry. Take Los Angeles retailer Fashion Nova. Its strategy of creating campaigns with celebrities such as rapper Cardi B and maintaining brand momentum through content produced by its network of approximately 3,000 Instagram influencers took it from being a small American retailer to one of the most searched brands on Google in 2017. It surrounded potential customers with digital content until it went from being five stores in southern California to being promoted by Kylie Jenner. In a 2018 interview with trade publication *WWD*, Fashion Nova CEO Richard Saghian refused to disclose profits but did reveal the company grew by 600 per cent in 2017.[3]

It was also a good year for Manchester-based online retailer Boohoo. In February 2017 – the company's year end – it announced profits had surged by 51 per cent following an aggressive influencer marketing campaign on Instagram in 2016. Neil Catto, Boohoo's chief financial officer, told *The Guardian* the retailer had worked with a 'spectrum' of influencers, from celebrities to bloggers, to grow awareness of its brand and products. 'It goes like wildfire on Instagram,' he said.[4]

However, it's not just fast, cheap products being shifted by influencers – higher ticket items also have added appeal thanks to their endorsement, or rather their ability to wear them in a way that is aspirational and relatable. Jennifer Dickinson, digital editorial director of Net-A-Porter, revealed street-style imagery featuring influencers drives more engagement than that of celebrities for the brand.

'We work with them for our street-style trend reports,' she says. 'When we started publishing these, we produced two a year but because of the difference they made when it comes to views and actual shopping, we now create one a month.'

Dickinson believes the positive impact of influencers on fashion brands comes from the fact their content is visually instructional.

'It's just great inspiration,' she says. 'I work in fashion, but I still need ideas on how to put things together – somebody to show me to roll up a sleeve or add jewellery. Influencers demonstrate how something can be wearable.'

But is monetization of the industry working?

In 2018 – on Instagram alone – there were 21.7 million sponsored influencer posts, according to Statista, which is a 10.6 million hike from 2017. The industry of digital influence has been aggressively monetized, is worth billions and only forecast to get bigger.

Yet the way in which it has been turned into a business is an uncomfortable reality for many of the actual influencers. Perhaps because it wasn't their idea, perhaps because they started their channels to have independent spaces in which they were the authority and brand deals ultimately mean they have several 'bosses' to answer to. Regardless of how it looks, dozens of interviews for this book have revealed the three parties involved in the monetization of digital influence – influencers, management and brands – have different goals. Influencers want to create content and get paid for it – they'll take the deals to continue doing what they love – but this is often approached as a necessary evil rather than part of a commercial master plan. Meanwhile, managers are either operating as ballsy opportunists or as suppliers to meet demand – they are fighting to create a market for their clients or delivering a commodity to an industry they were already operating in. And brands? Ultimately, they want to sell product. Period.

For some influencers, the chance they may lose the trust of their audience via existing ways to commercialize their work is too much of a risk – they won't do it. Musician and vlogger Tom Rosenthal rejects every brand deal that appears in his inbox. 'It would be such a turn-off if people saw me popping up holding a tin of beans,' he says. 'People are very delicate about things like this and it always has an air of desperation.'

As a creative influencer, Rosenthal has several routes to commercialization which allow him to work full-time on producing music and content. He has a publishing deal with record label Universal, started performing live in 2019 and has released several albums.

However, an increasing number of lifestyle influencers are rediscovering the entrepreneurial spirit that drove them to create content for their own channels rather than a traditional publisher and springboarding products they have created rather than promoting those made by other brands. Australian lifestyle blogger Elle Ferguson revealed her beauty range, Elle Effect, was so desired by the followers of her flagship Instagram that tens of thousands followed the Instagram dedicated to this new project before they even knew what it was. 'I started the page on a Saturday night at 6:30 pm in the lounge with my boyfriend,' she says. 'Three days later, I had 30,000 people following the account without actually knowing what I was selling. Those 30,000 people were customers wanting to buy something they hadn't tried and hadn't seen, but they wanted it.'

If influencers can create strong enough product propositions which simultaneously strengthen their own brand and allow them to avoid jeopardizing the trust of their audiences, do they need sponsorship and promotional content deals? As part of a long-term plan, it seems to follow, no.

Pentland isn't entirely critical of the monetization of the industry but does believe there is a significant job to be done when it comes to managing expectations and educating brands and agencies on what a commercial deal should look like if it is to result in compelling content.

'Partnerships would benefit from more open communication and less distance between the client and the creator,' she says. 'It's much better if I can talk to the brand or the agency – after all it's a two-way thing.'

Clarifying her position on how a brand should view an influencer partnership, she says: 'You're not buying ad space – you're renting a room at my party, not buying a billboard.'

Education is something that comes up time and time again, regardless of who you talk to in the industry. There is an anxiety that in the race to catch up or keep up, the same mistakes are being made repeatedly. Budgets aren't necessarily being spent in the most productive ways and this industry of digital influence – believed to be fast-paced and constantly evolving – is actually sitting still.

Barbour-Brown believes the idea the influencer marketing business is a progressive one across the board is a fallacy. He says: 'People will tell you it is always changing but when you go to events and meetings, the questions are always the same. That's down to lack of education and understanding.'

Although worrying, this presents an opportunity for brands to excel as there is – according to those at the heart of the industry – so much room for improvement. Current methods of monetization seem to be problematic. The influencer – who should be leading the process through sharing information and data about what their audience responds to in order to inform campaign direction – is expected to compromise their integrity and publish content that they may know will fail to catalyse engagement.

However, Pentland, Rosenthal and Ferguson are part of the early-adopting elite, who joined social media first, learned quickly, developed several streams of income and are now able to reap the benefits. The much larger truth about the influencer industry is most content creators struggle to monetize effectively and will not make millions from their social platforms. In fact, the vast majority are not turning down sponsorship deals and trying to school brands, but struggling to effectively commercialize even large audiences to a point where it is feasible for them to make a living from their content alone. The influencer industry does not deliver a lucrative career or luxury lifestyle indiscriminately – regardless of how it looks on social media. In saying that, it is in influencers' interests to give the impression of an aspirational setting, even if this does not reflect reality, to demonstrate to brands they are capable of providing a desired context for their products.

And Rosenthal is correct – creating sponsored content brings in cash but turns off audiences, as YouTuber Gaby Dunn revealed in her viral first-person piece for website Splinter in 2015, 'Get rich or die vlogging: The sad economics of internet fame'. When she published videos that had been facilitated by brand money, she lost subscribers and experienced a very public backlash from her audience, frustrated by any kind of commercialization and disappointed by her decision to try to monetize. She revealed she struggled to pay her rent, sold her clothes to make ends meet and doesn't believe this was something she could document on her social channels as, while 'authenticity' has been the buzzword of the industry since 2015, her audience does not want this on a daily basis. In the article, she stated pictures of her at brunch will get higher engagement than her 'searching for quarters'.

Although Zoe Sugg, PewDiePie and KSI are repeatedly namechecked in mainstream media's coverage of YouTubers making millions, they are exceptions. In fact, 96.5 per cent of YouTubers make less than $16,800 a year from the platform, according to a decade-long study by the Offenburg University of Applied Sciences in Germany. The most profitable route to getting a return seems to be via Instagram where brand deals are the smartest way to make money and value is attributed in a case-by-case basis but, even then, the wide variation on what influencers will accept means it would be inaccurate to say this is lucrative across the board. Most brands are still feeling their way financially and the absence of established standard pricing based on shared values means most influencers have very different experiences of monetization.

One person who understands the brand/influencer friction better than most is Lucy Nicholls, who has one foot in each camp of the industry. Not only is she a fashion blogger who set up her website Shiny Thoughts in 2009, she is also a social media content producer for British fashion brand Boden and in this role works with influencers. Alongside creating sponsored posts for her own platforms in partnership with brands, she is frequently tasked with commissioning influencers to do this as part of her day job.

Her advice? 'Brands need to understand the trust that exists between influencers and their audiences and that this is worth investing in.'

Meanwhile, having spent a year analysing and troubleshooting issues in the industry prior to launching his News UK-backed influencer agency THE FIFTH in 2019, Oliver Lewis believes the only route to change and a deeper sense of satisfaction for every party is longer-term, more substantial partnerships. However, he doesn't believe this can happen in a widespread way overnight. He says: 'Influencer marketing is one of the most exciting and fast-growing areas in brand communication, but it's still in its infancy.' He adds: 'As with any industry in rapid growth, challenges persist.'

His view on the route to a better business? 'Identifying the right talent, building longer-term partnerships, authenticating their background and proving meaningful ROI.'

Trust. Rigorous talent identification. Communication. It could be worse, right?

FROM INFLUENCER TO GURU: THE FASCINATING JOURNEY OF XJAWZ

SO, WHAT HAPPENED TO THE 'scruffy lad' Sam Betesh – AKA XJawz – who sparked Chivers' light-bulb moment in 2012 that digital entertainment was his future business? He went from being a YouTuber to becoming an influencer marketing expert for some of the world's most innovative companies – via Justin Bieber. He started his YouTube channel at the age of fifteen in 2009 and grew his subscriber base from zero to 80,000 in twelve months. At one point, he was the second most popular gamer on the platform renowned for his instructional videos on how to become a better Call of Duty player. Although this period was the foundation for an extraordinary career to come – after all, it made him one of the first stars of the platform – it is not one he recalls with happiness. 'It was very weird,' he says. 'I didn't have any friends at school so I didn't have anyone to share it with. I can't stress that enough. I didn't have a life and for five to seven years, I didn't have a single friend.' By the time he was eighteen, technology companies including HP and EA were flying him to promotional shoots where he'd meet fellow gaming YouTubers he'd previously only talked to on Twitter. 'It was nuts,' he admits. Having made two to three videos a day, he gave up YouTube for approximately seven months after making a friend he wanted to spend time with and realizing he was exhausted. 'I was kind of burned out,' he says. 'I was tired of making videos.' However, this didn't last for long. Soon after, he dropped out of college, made approximately 100 videos in a year and then quit the platform completely in 2012. 'There was a certain amount of anxiety about being a man child with no skills and not having a full life,' he says, although he believes he could have had the same level of success as gaming YouTuber Ali-A. 'He's an example of what I could have been.' A chance meeting with two guys who provided social media management for rappers at a party in San Francisco made him consider how musicians could use YouTube to share behind the scenes content. He pitched this to the guys he'd met at the party. By the end of 2012, they had started a company together and he was living in Los Angeles with one of them, brokering deals for influencers such as Bieber and Kylie Jenner.

In 2013, he experienced first-hand how willing brands were to spend money on influencer marketing thanks to his work with the teen idol and singer, who was travelling the world with his 'Believe' tour. He says: 'People know me as the YouTuber who disappeared and then reappeared in Miami with Justin Bieber – there was a lot of Bieber that year.' By Betesh's account, influencer marketing at this point was a much more chaotic, less managed process than it has become. Brands were throwing product at the star in return for social media promotion, while Airbnb gave Bieber and his entourage a £10,000-a-night mansion to party in. He says: 'I made sure he did an Instagram post about it in the final hour.' Betesh also moved in to Bieber's house for approximately one month while he was touring; however, this part of his career came to an end when the singer returned. 'He didn't want so many people living in his house,' he says. 'Plus $50K had gone missing.' Utilizing his skills, Betesh pushed himself as a influencer marketing guru and focused on consulting for technology and lifestyle brands such as Fabletics and Uber, where the budgets for these partnerships are enormous but so too is the return. His one piece of advice? 'Micro influencers really work.'

HOW TO MAKE A FORTUNE THROUGH ONE BRAND DEAL

DESPITE BEING BEST KNOWN FOR streaming his play of free game Fortnite: Battle Royale on Twitch, professional gamer Tyler Blevins – also known as Ninja – promoted the challenger to its throne, Apex Legends, in 2019 on Twitter and Twitch. The price tag for EA, the brand behind the partnership? A reported $1m. However, this could be regarded as money well spent – the game was downloaded 50 million times in February alone – the first month of its release – despite having no launch campaign.

KEY TAKEAWAYS

- The first generation of influencers, early-adopting YouTubers, are frequently expensive to work with due to the fact the first era of influencer managers are sales people and regard their clients' platforms and stories as a high-value commodity. This has the potential to be utilized, adapted and shaped by buyers but to do this, they must pay a premium. Their skills really lie in their ability to make deals happen, acting as gatekeepers to their talent and ensuring the value of what these individuals are selling is not compromised.
- Second-era managers are responding to demand for influencers in markets they were already operating in, having seen portions of marketing budget being dedicated to influencer marketing in a significant way since 2014. Many of these individuals come from media or traditional management backgrounds and therefore have an existing process for working with talent which they apply to influencers. Rather than breaking ground, they are focused on picking up briefs for influencer campaigns which – if they hadn't adapted – would have potentially gone to quicker moving competitors.
- Influencers would welcome the opportunity to educate and communicate more directly with brand partners rather than receive feedback on campaigns and creative via third parties. They would prefer to share insight into what their audiences engage with than produce work which they know is unlikely to be well received.

- Brands should not regard influencer channels as hard, direct sales platforms. Influencers are not selling display adverts but offering commercial partners the opportunity to have their products inserted into an aspirational or relatable lifestyle. Due to this, pushing for strict marketing messaging to be used instead of influencers' regular tone of voice stands to have a negative impact on the success of campaigns.

- Part of what brands are paying for is the trust between the influencer and their audience and they should approach this as a long-term investment rather than producing one-off ephemeral campaigns. A deeper partnership will allow them to capitalize on this trust and become a regular part of the influencer's story rather than just the money behind another sponsored post.

- For some influencers, producing sponsored content and being part of promotional campaigns is out of the question – they simply will not jeopardize the relationship they have with their audience by attempting to commercialize it.

- Those with established and passionate audiences are discovering they may not need brands to fund their content operations any more, having created and launched their own product lines. The ambitions of influencers are much greater than they were when the industry started to boom in 2014, meaning brands may have to become more persuasive too if they want them to be in their campaigns and gain access to their audiences.

- Want quick responses from influencers' managers? Every manager interviewed advises you include the following four pieces of information in your first email: the assets you need, your deadline, your messaging and your budget.

Notes

1   Susanne Ault, 'Survey: YouTube stars more popular than mainstream celebs among U.S. teens', *Variety*, 5 August 2014. Available at: https://variety.com/2014/digital/news/survey-youtube-stars-more-popular-than-mainstream-celebs-among-u-s-teens-1201275245/.

2   Emma Guns, 'Dom Smales: Gleam, belief & talent', 10 July 2018. Available at: http://emmagunavardhana.com/the-emma-guns-show/dom-smales-gleam-belief-talent.

3 Aria Hughes, 'How Fashion Nova won the internet', *WWD*, 28 February 2018. Available at: https://wwd.com/fashion-news/fashion-features/inside-fashion-nova-cardi-b-1202595964/.

4 Rupert Neate, 'Fashion retailer Boohoo nearly doubles profit after celebrity Instagram tie-ups', *Guardian*, 27 April 2017. Available at: https://www.theguardian.com/business/2017/apr/26/boohoo-profits-nearly-double-celebrities-instagram-online-fashion-retail.

4

Myspace, Facebook and YouTube: defining digital with UGC

The arrival of Myspace in 2003 and Facebook the following year changed consumers' online behaviour in a way that set up YouTube to be a fruitful space for influencer-produced entertainment. By the time the former had started to gather pace between 2007 and 2008, there was not just an appetite for user-generated content (UGC) but to those who had invested time in Myspace and Facebook, watching YouTube felt natural. No drama. No high production values. Just regular-seeming individuals with cameras and charisma in settings almost identical to that of their viewers. For xennials and millennials, publishing personal information on the internet had become commonplace and while culturally it had been accepted that Myspace was not a mainstream platform, Facebook most definitely was. Following the lives of friends, family and peers was the partial catalyst for 'second screen' behaviour – using one's smartphone or tablet while watching television – as minute-to-minute publishing and the desire to keep up with it became normal.

While Myspace arguably created and facilitated proximity to the first digital influencers, particularly up and coming musicians, Facebook unlocked the power of relatable content and the idea that sharing could result in the creation of a supportive online network. The former gave this new strand of internet celebrities a direct route to their fans, while the latter correctly hypothesized that people documenting the everyday – as an independent choice – could be the future of communication.

YouTube combined these two elements and moved social media forward by delivering watchable content that encapsulated both of these key things. The result? An influencer movement that was soon unstoppable.

It is worth noting, however, that Facebook has not played a mainstream role in the influencer industry mostly due to lack of brand commercial opportunities for content creators on the platform. Most of the interviewees for this book stated they pay little attention to growing an audience on Facebook, partially because it doesn't benefit them financially and partially because it is much harder to build a community there. For many who are working independently across several platforms, focusing on delivering content to existing audiences and demonstrating this content is successful is imperative to maintaining engagement, driving profit and short-term future-proofing. When it comes to these criteria, Facebook fails to tick any boxes for most but it has been making efforts, since around 2017, to create inroads with influencers – particularly in the gaming community – and has made progress here thanks to attracting big names who are skilled at live streaming. In addition, it is still a staple for digital publishers and news companies – albeit less effective since the Newsfeed algorithm change of 2018, which prioritized 'friends and family' content over that of brands and businesses.

While Myspace redesigned the music industry and Facebook normalized engaging with relatable content, YouTube exploded as the youth platform that very few people in mainstream media understood. Thanks to the passion of early adopters and their swift realization that collaboration could lead to significant audience growth, communities formed and the relationship dynamic was initially – and crucially – based on the content creator's desire to help their subscribers and have a creative outlet. Most early YouTubers will admit they didn't see their channels as a career route: in fact, for many it was something to do that provided light relief from a job they hated while figuring out what their true calling was. However, when their video views and the level of their audience's engagement became too voluminous to ignore, their efforts led to a wholly more interesting life than they thought possible. This is the early-adopter fairy tale – the YouTube of today versus that of their era is unrecognizable in its sprawl. As a result, many are anxious about its ultimate destination and uncertain over whether or not they want to be part of it.

Did traditional media see this new kind of publisher – individuals with cameras and charisma – coming? No. As Casey Neistat says in his now iconic 2017 YouTube video about content creators entitled 'Do what you can't': 'The haters, the doubters are all drinking champagne on the top deck of the *Titanic* and we are the fucking iceberg.'

Myspace and the first digital influencers

An early adopter of Myspace was interiors stylist, entrepreneur and blogger Sarah Akwisombe, but at that point she was better known as rapper and producer GoldieLocks. She joined the platform between 2004 and 2005 to share her music, and compares it to the way Instagram is now: if you were on it, you were obsessed and it was an essential part of growing rapidly. Referring to it as a 'bubble', she says: 'Everyone was building followers or whatever they called them then, checking how many plays their tracks had and how many comments were being left on their page.'

She adds: 'I got a manager through it, a publishing deal and loads of gigs all around the world.' Akwisombe also remixed music for ex-Sugababe Mutya Buena, as well as producing beats and writing for British stars of the time Kate Nash and Tinchy Stryder. Although it wasn't possible to monetize content on Myspace, as influencers can do on social platforms now, she describes the opportunities it provided as 'staggering'. 'I played gigs around Europe every weekend for about three years solid thanks to Myspace,' she says, having accumulated more than 22,000 followers on the platform.

Also prominent was Lily Allen, who started sharing her life, unfiltered opinions and music via the website in 2005. Like Akwisombe, she dropped new music there instead of through a record label and by the time traditional media had discovered her in 2006, she had accumulated nearly 25,000 'friends', something the *Observer* journalist Miranda Sawyer described at the time as 'staggering'.

In an interview with the publication that year, Allen encapsulated the appeal of influencers on social networks before the industry had even began to fully form, saying: 'I think the secret to the success of Myspace is that you're not being sold anything, and there's something really special about that.' She understood that the access and human interaction provided by the platform allowed her followers to feel part of her story and that nurturing this relationship was important.

As a music fan, early blogger and social media adopter Olivia Purvis – founder of website What Olivia Did – was an active member of Myspace and remembers that feeling connected to people and their stories at this point was really the appeal of joining. 'I think it was one of the first community-led platforms out there, which made everything from meeting like-minded people, to discovering new music really accessible and within reach,' she says.

It was also indicative of the world Myspace would become – something completely countercultural to the mainstream music industry, which at this point was still dominated by mystery and a relatively small number of bands that traditional media deemed to be important. These bands did not speak for themselves but through magazines like *Rolling Stone* and *NME*, and the difference between the musicians being featured there and those gathering followers and popularity on Myspace couldn't be more stark. While Florence Welch and Kate Nash were gaining traction on Myspace for their confessional, relatable pop songs, *Rolling Stone* was leading issues with Paul McCartney and Green Day.

At its peak in 2008, Myspace had amassed 75.9 million unique monthly users, including emergent celebrities such as Kim Kardashian West, Taylor Swift, Tom Hardy and Lana Del Rey, and was a comparative, mould-breaking success to its competitors Bebo and Friends Reunited. It seemed to encapsulate youth culture and was arguably the first place that people in their masses began to construct digital identities, expressing who they were through carefully posed pictures and music that reflected their tastes – the scene they considered themselves to be part of. In addition, it was its own world – one that traditional media barely touched upon and rarely seemed to understand.

But Myspace wasn't just the birthplace of celebrities who have since achieved global, mainstream fame; it was also where some of YouTube's first major content creators honed their skills and built their brands. For example, before his beauty vlogs made him one of the most influential people on the platform, Jeffrey Lynn Steininger, AKA Jeffree Star, was an aspiring musician and, by 2006, the most followed person on Myspace. He shared his latest work, which would gather thousands of comments, all prior to him signing with a record label and releasing his first song through traditional channels in 2009. Alongside this, Steininger posted videos of him defending himself in the face of homophobic abuse and, at a time when there were very clear celebrity archetypes that he did not adhere to, he was able to build his fanbase independently. Meanwhile, future YouTuber Shane Lee Yaw, better known as Shane Dawson, posted blogs and videos on Myspace and promoted his merchandise. In doing so, he became a digital heartthrob for a generation by creating the kind of content that now dominates YouTube, from talking about his latest 'layouts' (a common Myspacer preoccupation) to inconclusive rambles filmed in his bedroom. He also addressed his followers directly, encouraging them to comment on his content and send him messages on the platform – behaviour that is still intrinsic to the influencer/follower relationship of today.

The thing that united people who became influencers on Myspace, and utilized their popularity to build audiences on Twitter, YouTube and Instagram in the years to come, is that they understood the power of offering their followers proximity. They realized human interaction and a dynamic that resembled friendship made their followers feel like they were part of their story.

They became invested in it and pursued these relationships across different platforms because the influencers were the real draw rather than the platforms themselves. In a way, their followers were platform-agnostic from the start, as their loyalty lay with the individuals themselves and not the way in which they were distributing content. Experiencing this devotion perhaps explains why some early influencers at times during interviews seemed apathetic about what the next big platform would be – it doesn't matter because they know their audiences will follow them.

As a result, Myspace established and normalized digital proximity. It allowed early influencers to have a direct relationship with their followers and develop a style of broadcasting that would easily be replicated on YouTube. It was arguably the first springboard for the first influencers but was not the platform that made sharing content feel like natural behaviour for everyone. It did not turn everyday monotony into obsessively scrollable, interactive entertainment. It did not plant the seed that, potentially, anyone could be an influencer or anyone's life could be interesting to the masses.

That step towards the creation of the influencer industry belongs to Facebook, which arguably burst the Myspace bubble in 2008 when benchmarking media analytics company Comscore reported that Facebook had officially accumulated more users. Akwisombe doesn't remember the platform's decline happening quickly, saying it 'sort of just died out', but does recall Facebook's superior functionality and the buzz around Twitter as being major reasons for people jumping ship.

In an interview with the *Guardian* the same year, Myspace co-founder Tom Anderson said he had discovered why his platform's user base had stagnated via surveying people. The general consensus revealed it was difficult to use, perceived to be just for music and teenagers, and lacked privacy. In short, it wasn't for everyone – but Facebook was.

So where does Facebook fit into the influencer industry?

If following the daily lives of musicians on the internet was normalized by Myspace, then Facebook broadened this to include everyone. The powerful thing about the platform has always been the Newsfeed – the fact that users can see pictures from family weddings next to content from celebrities and news from media companies. The subtext? Everyone's story is important. However, it is this widespread adoption of sharing and reacting that made UGC's domination of much of the mainstream internet seem completely normal. Why not watch a YouTuber's birth story? After all, you've just seen intimate pictures of a friend's labour on Facebook. Above everything else, the platform initially communicated that normal people are fascinating and humans should celebrate this through watching and staying in touch. Therefore in an indirect way, mass adoption of Facebook assisted the normalization of online communities and the complete acceptance of non-mainstream celebrities as entertainment.

In terms of the influencer industry, however, Facebook has never been the primary platform of choice or, if it was, it simply served as a starting-off point. For example, modest fashion vlogger and entrepreneur Dina Torkia, also known as Dina Tokio, began sharing imagery on Facebook of clothes she'd made, before progressing to showcasing them on YouTube. Although she maintains this platform, she does not seem to create content specifically for it but instead most frequently publishes YouTube videos there and links to her other platforms.

Meanwhile, although many influencers have Facebook pages, they are not a priority for most. For any publisher – be it an influencer or a media brand – the appeal of the platform was always shareability and clickthrough. One could publish a link to a listicle about lipstick and see it go viral on Facebook within a few hours, driving thousands of people to their website. Millennial-focused media brands such as Refinery29, Buzzfeed and Elite Daily at one point based their entire strategy around creating relatable content aimed at a Facebook audience, which would share it with their friends and family. Media companies embracing the platform, particularly before the aforementioned algorithm change in 2018, were so invested in it (compared to influencers) due to the different ways each publisher makes money. While media companies were tasked with selling display advertising and commercial content on their websites and had to drive a certain number of unique visitors there to do this, the most lucrative way for influencers to make money has been through sponsored content on Instagram and YouTube. Therefore focusing on growing audiences and engagement in these places makes more sense for their business model than trying to do so on Facebook, as brands have been far less interested in the platform in the context of influencer campaigns.

However, this may not be the case forever and not all influencers have discounted the platform. For example, for vlogger and author Louise Pentland, Facebook is becoming a key space in which to publish and she has discovered that the crossover between this audience and those on YouTube and Instagram is surprisingly low. Meanwhile, the platform has also become a popular option for certain gaming live streamers – perhaps most prominently David Steinberg, also known as StoneMountain64, who has a major YouTube subscriber base as well but an exponentially more engaged audience on Facebook. In an interview with the platform in 2017, he said posting short videos helped increase the rate at which his content was being shared and noted his audience on there is friendliest, perhaps because followers engage using their personal profiles. 'It's amazing what happens when people comment as their true selves, without hiding behind a username or fake identity,' he said.

As far as Clemmie Telford – founder of Mother of All Lists, parenting Instagrammer and former Facebook employee – is concerned, the true influence on the platform can be found in its groups, particularly those which are 'secret' (invitation only) and operate as communities. A prime example of this is the phenomenally impactful FIN, previously called Female In Nigeria, which was started by Nigerian journalist Lola Omolola in 2015 in response to terrorist group Boko Haram's 2014 kidnapping of 276 girls from their school in Chibok. A private set-up, it has a membership of over one million women, who use the group to share stories about the issues they are facing and often harrowing experiences they have been through. However, there are rules members must follow to retain their membership: no judging fellow members and no religious advice. In an interview with the BBC in 2018, Omolola said: 'There were women who had been abused for forty years and hadn't told anyone. No one should live like that.'

Meanwhile, in the UK, if one is a female freelance journalist, being invited to Facebook group The No. 1 Freelance Ladies Buddy Agency is an immediate route to editors and actually getting commissioned. This also occasionally acts as a group therapy destination for freelancers frustrated with the industry as well as a place to crowdsource case studies for writers on tight deadlines.

Founder of the group, Jenny Stallard, remembers coming up with the idea for the group during a shift for a national newspaper in 2007. The aim was to create a virtual office for freelancers like herself where they could chat, network and openly discuss issues such as pay without fear of the world seeing. Pitching Hour – its Friday tradition in which freelancers post pitches for editors to review – is particularly popular, as it is an efficient way for the former to get work and the latter to fill space. Stallard notes that the reason the group is so influential is down to its members, who are a mix of 'staffers and freelancers', and its ability to facilitate people digitally crossing paths in a way which is mutually beneficial. The group now has six administrators and she admits that moderating the page alone could easily turn into a full-time job if she didn't have her own freelance career to focus on too. 'Daily challenges can range from someone reporting a post, to someone commenting on a post from a long time ago and sending it to the top of the feed,' she says. Potentially libellous comments and members being rude to each other are also a concern, and she notes that having rules within Facebook groups is 'essential'. She says: 'They give us a point of reference when we're moderating – we'll sometimes debate if a post should be approved and a rule can decide the yes or no.'

How first-generation YouTubers changed the internet

The early-adopting YouTubers – some of whom started channels as early as 2006 – shaped the internet, digital culture and online entertainment as we know it today. They were light years ahead of traditional media in their entrepreneurial approach to broadcasting and their realization that the audience must be part of the process.

As many of them gathered subscriber bases of hundreds of thousands, and eventually millions, anyone who wasn't in their world looked on with a mixture of disbelief, confusion and dismay. How was this new media happening? And why?

These days creators can earn millions of dollars a year from their channels – according to Statista, the platform was most lucrative for kids' channel Ryan ToysReview ($22m), Jake Paul ($21.5m) and sports entertainment channel Dude Perfect ($20m) in 2018 – but it seems to be a universal truth among early adopters that money wasn't the point when they started. And that's not because they were independently wealthy – in fact, many came from humble backgrounds and put so much time into the platform because there was something about this mode of communication and the community that just clicked for them. Eman Kellam, who started his channel 'for fun' in 2012, admits it wasn't about the 'views or the money' but producing content like-minded people could enjoy.

YouTuber and author Louise Pentland says: 'We didn't set out to create this, we just liked making videos and having an open dialogue with people.'

The interaction between creators and their subscribers was key from the start. In a 2015 interview with *Rolling Stone* magazine, Felix Kjellberg – also known as PewDiePie – revealed his decision to humorously run from danger in horror video games was due to doing it once while playing Amnesia and his audience's immediate positive response.

Meanwhile Patricia Bright started making friends online via forums and this led to her starting a YouTube channel. 'I was really interested in skincare and hair and commenting on this with other girls who were into that as well,' she explains. 'We were typing to each other and then started sending videos to each other using YouTube.'

For Jana Hisham – sixteen years old when she started her channel in 2010 – the fact she could connect with people all over the world was too enticing not to get involved. 'I was enchanted by the idea of being able to reach like-minded individuals, express my opinions and have interesting discussions,' she says. 'I felt it was a unique experience where otherwise we would be total strangers, sometimes thousands of miles apart.'

That's not to say growth came easily or quickly. Joe Sugg worked long days as a roof thatcher for his uncle's business and created content for YouTube in the evenings. He didn't quit his job until he had 1.6 million subscribers. Marcus Butler was a software salesman and Jim Chapman was doing an insurance role he hated. YouTube was a place for escape – somewhere to build a passion project – but at the time of the early adopters, it was undervalued and misunderstood. In fact, people were so broadly derogatory about it that Bright, who was interning in investment banking at the time, admits she initially kept her channel a secret.

'I was embarrassed that I did it,' she says. 'I didn't think it seemed like a smart thing to do – there was no way I'd tell my boss I was filming what I bought when I went shopping.' When colleagues discovered her channel, she immediately shut it down. 'It sounds so bad to say this now but I was really ashamed.' However, that shame did not last for long as the industry of YouTube started to gather traction between 2010 and 2012 before content creators as a cultural phenomenon exploded in 2013.

It became clear that during the years they had spent exploring and building in this 'wide open space', as Pentland calls it, they became a significant and immovable part of not just digital but youth culture. Their content formats – hauls, chatty vlogs and let's play games – were raking in more views than many traditional media outlets could dream of online. The platform itself still felt so experimental that there was no reason not to try something new and the fact it was so community-based rather than entertainment-focused meant there was a sense of safety in exploring how one could express their creativity and discovering what caught fire. The platform attracted people who wanted to have complete autonomy over what their channel was for. This is summed up by Casey Neistat's aforementioned video, 'Do what you can't'. In a monologue over clips featuring himself and others on the platform, he says: 'When you're a creator, you don't need someone in your ear telling you want you can and can't do.'

YouTuber Taha Khan started watching content online in 2007 and created his current channel in 2013 when the platform had just hit one billion users. Despite this milestone, he remembers feeling like it was a close-knit thing to be part of. 'The whole of YouTube was kind of one community,' he says.

By this point, Pentland admits she was 'completely consumed' by the platform. 'I'd made friends with other people who were vlogging and all of my socializing revolved around it. I was living and breathing it.'

A communal obsession seems to have been key in building the world of YouTube. Everyone interviewed adores talking about the period from 2012 to 2014, when their channels started to boom and their work online began to seep into their lives offline. Although Bright's first commercial partnership was with New Look, she knew – even then – that beauty would be her niche.

By this point, she was successfully navigating her career in finance while editing videos every weekend – and this dual existence was beginning to pay off. 'I started getting offered more and more work and bigger campaigns but I couldn't do them because of my job. Things just progressed.'

Pentland describes this boom period as 'crazy' and 'unbelievable'. 'I still can't believe it,' she says. She recalls walking the red carpet at the premiere of One Direction's film *This Is Us* with Alfie Deyes, Zoe Sugg and Marcus Butler. 'There were just so many screaming teenagers. We had to be hidden beforehand – it was 2013 and YouTube had gone nuts. Teenagers just loved it – it was their thing. I still can't believe what it was like back then, it was the craziest world.'

Indeed, the crowd reaction at that particular event when the group – along with Jim Chapman and Tanya Burr – appear on the red carpet is so intense, so extreme that Sugg's vlog documenting the experience is difficult to watch because her hands are shaking so much.

Interview any of these YouTubers who were there then and there is a sense that this was the golden age of the platform. It was less complicated, more community-focused and something to be proud of. Having relentlessly built this online world, dedicated their time to it and taken seriously the desires of their followers, they were able to finally enjoy the fruits of their labour.

Although Pentland says everything was trial and error – there wasn't a lucid strategy that made YouTube explode – she is clear that her actions on the platform were not passive. 'I wasn't going with the tide, we came before that. In fact, we started the tide,' she says. It is this independent spirit and innate entrepreneurialism that allowed YouTube to become such an integral part of the internet. The early YouTuber mindset is so different from that of influencers who started their careers on other platforms. Their aim was to build something completely new based on their personal view about what was entertaining and would be useful to their audiences. In comparison, Instagram influencers often cite lack of representation in mainstream media as their reason for embarking on independent publishing – there was a gap in the market and they wanted to plug it. But for early YouTubers, traditional media was not part of their thought process – they were not bouncing off its failures or attempting to create a better alternative to what it was offering. It cannot be overestimated how focused these individuals were on building something completely different, which was utterly brand new. Bright sums it up succinctly: 'I wasn't looking for someone else to represent me – I chose to represent myself.'

Audience growth, collab culture and its legacy

Delivering content in a supply-and-demand style off the back of what their audiences liked or expressed a desire to see was a key reason why early YouTubers were able to grow their subscriber bases. But this was also down to creators seeking each other out, developing friendships in real life and appearing on everyone's respective channels. For example, Caspar Lee and Troye Sivan first met on Skype and became friends in 2011. By 2013, they were staying in a house in Los Angeles with Jack Harries, Louis Cole, Pentland and Joe Sugg to name a few of the definitive content creators of the time.

As explained in Chapter 2, this led to the formation of ecosystems in which everyone would cross-promote their friends, thus assisting their audience's discovery of their content which inevitably led to spikes in subscriber numbers for each influencer.

Friendships began in the early days through meet-ups, a practice today's YouTubers are still invested in although more so to meet their fans. Meet-ups are now also a commercial opportunity and often sponsored by brands if they are keen to bring a specific audience into their stores. However, in the first era of YouTube these were entirely focused on community engagement, and were both frequent and spontaneous. Pentland says: 'They started because there were little gatherings popping up all over the place to meet the people who watched your videos. As things got bigger, there were too many people to do this any more.'

At this point, American YouTubers, authors and brothers Hank and John Green, known for their collaborative channel Vlog Brothers, founded VidCon, an annual conference for content creators and their fans at which there were panels on issues relevant to the world of YouTube and opportunities to have meet-ups. This led to transatlantic meet-ups and the start of collab culture, in which producing videos with fellow YouTubers became a frequent, global practice. 'That was how everyone grew their audiences in the early days,' says Pentland.

This strategy has been adopted by many successful influencers, from Jake Paul with his controversial YouTuber collective Team 10 to gaming team Sidemen and Jamie Oliver, whose channel is now eponymous but launched as FoodTube and was defined by its collaborations. These included cooking tutorials by YouTubers such as Katie Pix and Jemma Wilson, the latter known online as Cupcake Jemma.

For Scott Major, founder of Minecraft-focused gaming channel DangThatsALongName, collaborating with fellow YouTubers was key to ensuring cut-through on the platform. He says: 'Back then Minecraft was at its peak, which meant it was a very saturated market. There was a lot of luck involved in managing to build a community within that. I was fortunate enough to have friends who also made videos on Minecraft, so we were able to create our own community, which viewers seemed to love.'

Collaborations reflected real-life friendships, accelerated audience growth and produced interesting content – which makes complete sense, right? But according to YouTuber Hisham, this culture – which started to turn sour in 2014 due to a number of creators being accused of abusing the adoration of their young audiences – has led to the platform being characterized by cliques, rather than inclusion. 'We saw a recoil from creators who started to recognize the negative impact of being associated with such a large group of people whose actions were very public and were constantly subjected to public scrutiny,' she says.

On top of this, Hisham observes, YouTubers represented by early-mover Dominic Smales' influencer management company Gleam Futures began to break away from the rest of the creator community and only work with each other. She describes Gleam's capitalization on this collaborative culture as 'profound', and that creators' realization of their financial worth as collaborators rather than seeking to be part of YouTube's community tended to create in-crowds. Due to this, she believes the platform has stagnated, as without the non-discriminatory collaboration that previously occurred, it is much harder for new talent to break through.

She notes that the fact these influencers lives are so fantastical now in comparison to when they started is also off-putting and has resulted in 'a lack of creative and engaging content'.

Although complimentary of YouTube's efforts to support creators, Hisham believes it must address this atmosphere of exclusion if the platform is to grow creatively and produce new talent. 'I think what they've failed to do is build robust communities which not only support each other but also are constantly welcoming newcomers,' she says. 'There seems to be a lack of willingness from industry and creators alike to seek out new talent and to nurture a truly collaborative attitude.'

One platform, many anxieties

Having started from such a gung-ho, positive place, YouTube now seems to be a platform that its first-generation creators are determined to rely upon less. Diversification is a key strategy, with many moving further into traditional media, writing, independent projects and offline brand collaborations, while maintaining their original YouTube audience, albeit through posting content less frequently.

Influencer manager Si Barbour-Brown says: 'It's about taking a multiplatform approach. My guys don't want to be forty and still doing vlogs – they want to be actors, television personalities and writing books.' He adds: 'They all have other talents but keep their channels going because there are times when things are not as busy.'

Throughout interviews and research for this book, 'still vlogging at forty' appears to be the first-generation YouTuber horror story – the thing they are most keen to avoid – which might explain why so many are attempting to gain traction elsewhere. Speaking on Marcus Butler's podcast Lower Your Expectations, in 2018, Jim Chapman revealed that YouTube is now the smallest part of his career and that filming a video in which Joe Sugg waxed his armpits in 2014 prompted him to embark on a 'coming of age' which involved building out his career to include writing and fashion. Since then, he admitted he has felt less like 'a performing monkey'. Referring to the video in question, he said: 'I thought, "That's going to do loads of views but I'm a bit embarrassed".' Using YouTube to create off-platform opportunities has also been the result of recognizing the limitations of his channel, which is ironic given how limitless YouTube seemed to him and fellow early adopters at the start of their journey. On the podcast he voiced the concern: 'What happens in five years time when you get to thirty, as I am, and your audience hasn't grown up with you?' He also said he has worked free of charge to get projects he is passionate about, and with brands he loves, off the ground.

A great deal of YouTuber anxiety also seems to come from uncertainty around the direction in which the platform is moving and the precarious reality of building a career entirely in a space that does not belong to them. 'If YouTube suddenly ceases to exist, it's the end of many careers,' highlights Barbour-Brown.

It may seem far-fetched, but platforms shutting down is not beyond the realms of possibility, and YouTubers often reference the closure of Vine in 2017 as proof that they simply cannot assume this won't happen. 'Vine was one of the biggest and influential platforms back in its day so its sudden closure was a very big surprise to myself and a lot of other creators,' explains Eman Kellam. 'Loads of my friends were solely based on Vine and they lost their careers when it closed down.' He reacted to this by growing social audiences on other platforms and starting to work on television projects with the BBC.

Meanwhile, Louise Pentland has been building an off-YouTube career since 2015 when her first book – a lifestyle guide called *Life with a Sprinkle of Glitter* – was published and became a *Sunday Times* bestseller. In 2017, she moved into fiction and has since written a trilogy of books around a protagonist, Robin Wilde. 'I'd got divorced, been on the dating scene and was living this single mum life,' she says, explaining why she decided to do more work in traditional publishing. 'I had credibility thanks to the success of the first book but I said to my publisher, I don't want this to be a blogger book, just a book in its own right.'

Like her peers, she also feels the need to have a back-up plan as the destiny of YouTube is not in her hands. 'You don't know where it is going to go, and what if one day it goes away?'

On the flipside of this worry about the platform's future, there is a definite sense of disappointment over the direction it has moved in as it has grown. Early-adopting YouTubers created something they are proud of, but the context in which that now lives is not something they are entirely comfortable with.

Khan believes the platform has to be seen as a place of multiple identities if one is to accept and understand it today, something he believes users who joined in that 2013 boom are not always willing to do. 'Talking about YouTube as one entity is not recognizing where YouTube is now. There's so much bad happening, that if you do that you'll only see the bad.'

Regardless of what you define as good or bad, every content creator interviewed – unlike Instagrammers, podcasters and bloggers – acknowledged that the platform has changed, and this means they must change too.

'I don't love it as much as I used to,' says Bright. 'It used to be community-focused and now it's about entertainment. That's the way the world is, nothing stays the same.'

The fact is that YouTube is now a sprawling platform in which the most dramatic videos seem to gain the most attention. Bright's assessment that it is more entertainment-focused is correct. Ironically, as traditional broadcasters attempt to adopt YouTube-style, gamified formats to ensure their content has a greater chance of going viral – James Corden's Carpool Karaoke is a good example of this – many digital creators are producing long-form work which is more akin to television. While Shane Dawson released a series of documentaries in 2018 about fellow YouTubers – most prominently Jake Paul – media startup Kyra TV is specifically focused on creating formats that viewers watch at the same time every week.

Kellam agrees. 'YouTubers want to be celebrities and celebrities want to be YouTubers. Slime videos. New trends always happen. You've got to evolve or get left behind.'

HOW YOUTUBE WORKS WITH INFLUENCERS

SINCE DEVELOPING ITS PARTNER PROGRAMME in 2007, YouTube has been nurturing content creators who demonstrated dedication and traction, meaning that anyone who racks up over 4,000 watch hours each year and has more than 1,000 subscribers is eligible to earn money via advertising on the platform.

In addition, the platform offers different opportunities to creators based on the size of their subscriber base: 100,000 subscribers or more makes influencers eligible for the Silver and Up tier, which gives them access to production spaces and facilities globally at which they can film content and host events. They can also be assigned a partner manager, who helps them grow their business on the platform, and are invited to exclusive YouTube events. Those in the Bronze tier (10,000 to 100,000 subscribers) can also use dedicated production spaces and are invited to enter its Next Up competition, which gives winners access to a five-day creator camp, means to buy new equipment and Silver and Up tier perks. Meanwhile, Opal (1,000 to 10,000 subscribers) and Graphite (zero to 1,000 subscribers) have access to online tutorials on growth-hacking and production.

Leona Farquharson, global lead for YouTube content creators, works directly with the platform's most prolific influencers to hone their strategies and help them to meet their goals. She says: 'Many of the creators we work with are developing wider media businesses around their content and brand, leveraging the loyalty and passion of their large fan base to tell their stories in creative and innovative ways.'

Despite describing creators as 'the lifeblood' of the platform, Farquharson says the company doesn't find new talent but is instead focused on growing existing influencers. 'We don't recruit creators, but rather support their growth,' she says. 'We support and encourage creators of all levels by offering benefits and opportunities tailored to fit their channel's specific level.'

THE UNCONVENTIONAL YOUTUBE STAR

MUSICIAN TOM ROSENTHAL WAS NEVER going to be a daily vlogger or fit in to mainstream YouTube culture. However, he did see how the platform could benefit independent creatives and utilized it to build the kind of career he wanted to have. This didn't include going down any route that featured a record label. 'I hate authority and people getting involved in my process,' he says. 'Also, a good manager can do the same thing as a record label quite comfortably.'

One of the things he wanted to do was make a video for every single song he wrote and have creative freedom to do this in a way he chose. The result is a disarmingly brilliant and unexpected body of work. In *Watermelon*, he dances through the countryside dressed as a watermelon, while *Melania* – in which he beseeches America's First Lady to leave President Trump – is a series of illustrations on a glittery background. In other videos, he simply sits at the piano in his home and plays. For him, the aesthetics often come first. 'From early on, I saw the importance of the visual aspect of songs,' he says. 'I enjoy making videos and I thought visually representing the songs was a crucial part of what I do.'

After his music took off, he started making series of vlogs featuring his work, conversations with his young daughters and reactions to his work. These videos are gently observational and sentimental rather than performative – nothing appears to be set up for his audience's entertainment – making them a welcome relief on a platform which can feel dominated by drama, high energy and clickbait. 'Vlogging felt like a personal leap but I've got a nice platform and it's nice to show a family,' he says.

Due to having multiple streams of revenue which come from his music, YouTube is not his livelihood and nor would he want it to be, despite hundreds of thousands of people subscribing to his channel. He admits the process required by professional YouTubers in which they have to chase trends to get visibility on the platform's homepage holds no appeal for him – he would rather produce work which he believes in, regardless of what's happening in other parts of YouTube.

'Good things stay good forever,' he says. 'Sometimes one of my old videos will suddenly gain new life. It doesn't matter that I made it in 2012.' He adds: 'I want to make things that last for a long time – that's always been my general way of doing things.'

THREE ECOSYSTEMS THAT BUILT YOUTUBE'S STARS

Team 10: the influencer incubator started by controversial star Jake Paul, who is the younger brother of equally divisive creator Logan Paul. The YouTuber moved several creators into a house in Los Angeles, providing them with equipment and brand deals to produce videos round the clock. However, the group were roundly mocked by the YouTube community when they released an original song 'It's Everyday Bro' in 2017 and were later the subject of mainstream news when several members left, claiming the Team 10 house had been toxic.

The Brit crew: also dubbed 'Team Gleam' because the majority are or were previously managed by Gleam Futures and composed of the early-adopting YouTubers including Zoe Sugg, Jim Chapman, Tanya Burr and Marcus Butler. These creators became friends in real life and saw how collaborating on content could accelerate their collective growth when YouTube was still a relatively open space.

The Sidemen: a group of YouTubers including Simon Minter, KSI, Vik Barn and Joshua Bradley who started gaming together online in 2013 and built out a brand from this which has included a television programme for Comedy Central, *The Sidemen Experience*, and merchandise. They also created a series for YouTube Premium in 2018 called The Sidemen Show.

KEY TAKEAWAYS

- The first digital influencers arguably came out of Myspace, although they tended to be emergent musical artists. There was no established way to monetize the platform, but having a prominent presence and significant following led to other lucrative opportunities. In addition, early Myspace content is very similar to what would become popular on YouTube, and several of the most popular YouTubers began building their audiences on Myspace.

- Although Facebook has not been a particularly appealing proposition to influencers due to the lack of brand opportunities that include the platform, this may change as it can deliver an older audience and a more engaged one than YouTube when it comes to video.

- The YouTube golden era was between 2012 and 2014, when content creators began to monetize and the power of the audiences they commanded began to be recognized.

- Early adopters of YouTube accelerated their growth through collaborating with fellow creators and cross-promoting content. These collaborations were often born out of real-life friendships, but accusations that some YouTubers were abusing the trust of younger audiences led to widespread collaborations ending and the community becoming less inclusive.

- The present and future of the platform is the source of much anxiety for some creators as they have seen it change so dramatically since 2015. They have addressed this by diversifying into mainstream media, writing books and exploring content formats more suitable for older audiences.

- YouTube is not one world but encapsulates thousands of communities, and referring to or thinking of it as one entity does not help one understand the platform – these communities, in many cases, exist independently of each other.

5

Twitter and breakdown of the authoritative media

It was February 2009 and Stephen Fry was stuck in an elevator at Centre Point, a landmark building in London. This relatively minor incident resulted in global media coverage – not because the actor was in serious danger nor that the events that led to this, or those that followed, were particularly dramatic. The interesting thing was that he had decided to document his predicament on Twitter. He wrote, to his then 100,000 followers: 'Ok. This is now mad. I am stuck in a lift on the 26th floor of Centre Point. Hell's teeth. We could be here for hours. Arse, poo and widdle.' And while hundreds responded with messages of support and ideas of how he might escape, Fry kept them updated with tweets on engineers' progress and his eventual liberation. Meanwhile, articles about the incident started to pop up online. Not just from UK media outlets, but from those in Australia and New Zealand too. Bloggers hypothesized that 'Stuck in a Lift with Stephen Fry' could easily be a brilliant television show. And all of this was instigated and perpetuated by the actor.

This signalled an early shift in the mechanics of reporting within traditional news companies. Rather than journalists exclusively breaking stories about individuals of note, or generating copy based on paparazzi pictures and gossip, the news was coming directly from individuals themselves. Media companies were being fed an agenda based on the numerical popularity and real-time impact of tweets, instead of setting it themselves: if a tweet was going viral, this indicated that it deserved attention. Individuals categorically owned their narrative and their willingness to share their lives in a bite-sized format began to have a ripple effect across the internet. Google Trends data shows searching for content about 'Stephen Fry lift' emerged and spiked at almost exactly the same time as his tweets started to gain traction. Desire for reportage on the incident didn't peter out until four months later. Despite being able to follow the action live and directly on the actor's Twitter feed, this search volume proved people still wanted context and longer format reportage on the incident – no matter that it was a regurgitation of Fry's tweets and sparse conjecture.

Fry certainly wasn't the first celebrity to use Twitter, but he was an early adopter and his decision to document his lift experience on the platform proved how powerful people – as opposed to media brands – owning their narrative on a global stage could be. Fellow early adopters included Ashton Kutcher, Oprah Winfrey, Justin Bieber, Barack Obama, Lady Gaga and Katy Perry. But it was Fry who showed that Twitter allowed celebrities to become digital influencers by inviting their followers into the most intimate, most everyday situations – situations which, previously, would have remained unreported and personal. He showed how the positioning of traditional media – the news-breakers – could be turned on its head by offering his fans a direct line to him. Twitter launched in 2006, but this moment demonstrated the power over global communications it offered the individual, through giving them the means to share independent minute-to-minute reportage.

However, Twitter remains very much a platform for a certain type of influencer, unlike Instagram, which one could argue has become an essential part of every content creator's output to ensure the optimization of their commercial potential. In fact, those who have significant followings on Twitter are more driven by its power to propel them and their ideas into mainstream media than obtaining brand deals or directly increasing their income. Opinions are their currency, and their ability to make these speedily and succinctly is the way in which they demonstrate their influence. It's not about being the most beautiful, extravagant, well-dressed, authentic or honest individual; it's about being the cleverest, most controversial or extreme voice to the extent that other users have an almost primal instinct to react.

Twitter's evolution into the platform it is today, and the kind of influencers it produces, can largely be attributed to what it takes to grow an audience there and to its users' addiction to the pacy, adrenaline-fuelled, call-and-response dynamics between them and those who follow them. As journalist and prolific meme-maker Mollie Goodfellow says: 'Every so often I think about quitting but I need the attention online.'

No other platform provides the discourse rally of Twitter and the way in which influence manifests here is completely different from Instagram, YouTube and Facebook. The value of a tweet is attributed based on how far and how quickly it can travel. In addition, given how frequently the platform is consulted – rightly or wrongly – by traditional media to take a snapshot of public reaction to significant events in the news, Twitter actually gives individuals the ultimate opportunity to define the narrative, and to give major happenings a tone of voice. The fact that large swathes of influential people from the worlds of media and politics are so invested in it means it punches significantly above its weight in terms of how much attention it manages to command. After all, at the end of 2018 it had just 321 million users, which is a fraction of the other mainstream platforms from its generation of social media – Facebook, YouTube and Instagram.

Can brands utilize Twitter's kind of digital influence in any meaningful way? It's certainly not impossible – in fact, companies who use the platform to speak truth to power, or can create content for it with both subtle and explicit humour, tend to reinforce their likeability. Take Burger King and its response to Kanye West tweeting, in 2018, that his favourite restaurant was McDonald's, which was: 'Explains a lot.' This was liked over one million times and went viral. Meanwhile – in reflection of its famous secret recipe including six herbs and five spices – the only people KFC follow on the platform are the five members of the Spice Girls and six men called Herb.

Can brands utilize influencers in this space? Only if they want to be associated with those who are leading and defining conversations that will potentially end up grabbing the attention of the mainstream media, because Twitter is all about the power of the individual's voice and how it can be used to draw out the emotions of many. But capturing its very specific strand of influence is tricky and understanding it more complex than anything that exists on any other platform.

How does influence work on Twitter?

Ideas, conversation, debate… Influence on Twitter is less about selling and promoting products and more about spreading a point of view, which is part of the reason why it presents fewer brand commercial opportunities for people with large social followings. In fact, everyone interviewed for this book who works in influencer management said none of their clients are even trying to monetize their Twitter feeds – the platform is not one they consider to be interesting from a business perspective. However, despite the fact that spreading ideas and opinions is the most effective way to use the platform, those who have accumulated significant audiences, and share their points of view several times on a daily basis, question how influential they actually are due to the existence of echo chambers. Hugo Rifkind – a columnist and writer for *The Times* – joined Twitter in 2009 and began using it as an 'interactive notebook', rather than something that might help progress his career or allow him to become more influential. 'It wasn't important in my office at all,' he says.

A decade on – and despite having tens of thousands of followers who retweet his work and thoughts – he has doubts over the idea that his seeming popularity on the platform makes him an influencer. In fact, he believes if he has a chance of having influence anywhere, it's in the print media for which he writes.

'I wouldn't say I'm an influencer because I think it's pretty rare that I will change someone's mind on Twitter,' he says. 'As a columnist for *The Times*, I think it's more likely people who don't agree with me will read my writing there and perhaps it might make them think.' He adds: 'With Twitter, there's definitely a sense of preaching to the converted.'

Despite this instinct, he has tried to marshal his following, namely to back Charity: Water, a non-profit organization that works to provide people in developing countries with clean, safe drinking water, a group that he has supported for several years. But sharing information about how others could help on Twitter had little effect.

'I thought, if I tweet about it loads, surely it will get some traction but maybe five or six people retweeted my tweets,' he says. 'I can have a bit of an impact but people will ignore you in a heartbeat.'

Fellow journalist and author Dan Hancox – a prolific commentator on music, social movements and gentrification for publications in the UK and America – agrees with Rifkind. Although he is frequently part of political and current affairs-focused debates on the platform, he doubts this has a real-life effect. He says: 'I think the number of people following me on Twitter who live in swing constituencies and will change who they vote for based on what I think is probably zero.'

Rifkind and Hancox's shared instinct about the limitations of their influence is correct. The platform's ability to create polarizing echo chambers, which give the impression that the majority point of view held within their bubble is the dominant one overall, was confirmed by Twitter's founder Jack Dorsey in a 2019 interview with *Rolling Stone*. 'We definitely help divide people. We definitely create isolation. We definitely make it easy for people to confirm their own bias,' he said.

However, despite the widespread view that the platform is 'the media talking to itself', Hancox argues there are still 'battles to be fought and won' there, primarily because making a point via Twitter can effectively springboard someone into the mainstream broadcast, print and digital media. Like Rifkind, Hancox believes this is where one can have genuine influence, and he has experienced how being prolific on the platform is a route to these stages. This is the case more than ever since the results of the UK general election in 2017, which signified much greater support for left-wing politics than the mainstream news companies had thought was possible. 'It showed how out of touch people in key positions of power in the media had become,' he says. Hancox admits he is frequently approached by editors because of thoughts he has shared on Twitter, and has seen the platform elevate individuals – who previously would not have been approached – to mainstream media opportunities, 'where the wider public are actually listening'.

However, there is one person who manages to shatter echo chambers again and again, and is able to insert their view into the consciousness of a wider audience: US president, Donald Trump. Rifkind explains: 'The right of politics and some bits of the hard left are very good at playing to the crowd. They don't just say what their followers want to hear but their opponents are so shocked they have to talk about it.' He adds: 'In this way, Trump defines both sides of the argument.'

Indeed, the US president's ability to deflect and distract, not just the Right but the Left and everyone in between, has revealed him – or perhaps his digital strategists – to be puppetry masters of the media's narratives, using Twitter as their most effective tool. Consider First Lady Melania Trump's visit to see children separated from their parents and detained at the Texas–Mexico border in June 2018, wearing a jacket emblazoned with the words: 'I really don't care, do u?' While her supporters on Twitter applauded this move, which she later said was aimed at the left-wing media (she claims it is obsessed with her wardrobe), the left-wing media duly responded with an excess of outraged comment pieces. Suddenly Melania's jacket was the story of the day, rather than the vulnerable children she was visiting.

The team behind the president, his family and digital strategy seem to understand that to create a hard-hitting narrative on Twitter, one must appeal to users' most basic emotions. 'That's how things go viral,' says Michael Wendling, BBC broadcast journalist and author of *Alt-Right: From 4chan to the White House.* 'Either you totally agree in a way that makes you feel joyful or it makes you angry and upset enough to comment and share.'

The alt-right, as a political movement, are skilled at using Twitter to feed stories to, and thus influence, the mainstream media and, in fact, approach it almost as a sport. However, Wendling highlights that this group is not being mobilized on Twitter but in darker parts of the internet – they are simply using the platform to aggravate and control the agenda of the left wing. 'Twitter is the mechanism for delivery rather than the root of the problem,' he says, citing the platform as the final stop for offensive discriminatory material in a journey that goes via 8chan, 4chan and Reddit before reaching Twitter and often Facebook. 'The alt-right hate mainstream media, but they love it when they get its attention,' says Wendling.

On the subject of American politics, one person who understands what it feels like to be catapulted from relative obscurity to an international stage is writer Mollie Goodfellow, who was one of the original Barack Obama and Joe Biden 'bromance' meme creators in 2016, following the election of Donald Trump.

The basic premise of these is while Obama is gracious about leaving the White House, Biden is intent on sabotaging the incoming president. Although thousands of memes circulate on Twitter every day – mainly thanks to this content format's popularity with the youth audience – these ones broke through into mainstream media and offered light relief at a time of widespread anxiety over what the future would look like, post-Obama.

Goodfellow explains: 'I was working for Sky News and was there on the night Donald Trump won the election. Everyone was so shocked – it felt like the worst thing that had ever happened. We realized Obama was actually leaving and I just felt like I needed to make everything a bit less shit.'

In Goodfellow's original meme – which she shared on Twitter that night – Biden is furious about Trump's victory while Obama is humorously diplomatic. This was retweeted 60,000 times. 'People really responded to it and some created their own versions too,' she says. 'The size of the response actually broke my phone. Then people from news networks started calling and asking if they could talk about my memes.' Since then, this genre of meme has become such a recognizable part of post-Obama digital culture that the former president himself even tweeted one to his former vice president on his birthday in 2017.

Since going viral, Goodfellow has seen her career as a comedy writer, meme-maker and journalist take off to the extent that she has written for comedian Frankie Boyle and the BBC current affairs panel show *Have I Got News for You*. However, describing the success of this style of content and why it has been so impactful on Twitter, she simply says: 'Memes are just really funny and people like funny.' She describes them as 'shorthand' for explaining or ridiculing situations. 'All you need is that perfect picture,' she adds and highlights that as fervour around meme culture has grown – in which sharing clever ones can result in serious audience growth – so too has the need to understand the cultural moments to which they refer. As an example of this, she cites the 2018 Netflix show *Bird Box* – which is set in a post-apocalyptic world where a mysterious force drives people to suicide – due to the fact that a high volume of memes began circulating Twitter almost at the same time as the show was released. 'It went so big on social that people were watching it to understand the memes,' she says. 'That's a new concept.' She adds that memes are simply how younger generations communicate due to their ability to help spread an idea quickly, and she believes they are – as a content format – here to stay.

However, being prolifically political on Twitter isn't always as straightforward as stating an opinion, starting a debate and then have the ideas within
this spreading. For some people in less liberal societies, who are deemed
too influential, there have been serious consequences following their views
gathering momentum and there have been efforts to silence them as a result.

One example of this is how the platform was used in the lead up to Pakistan's
general election in 2018. Ahead of this, the country's three main political
parties – Pakistan Muslim League (Nawaz) (PML-N), Pakistan Peoples Party
(PPP) and Pakistan Tehreek-e-Insaf (PTI) – had developed social media cells
into which they fed their messaging through key influencers, who backed their
policies and criticized their opponents.

'So far, so standard,' says journalist Issam Ahmed, who was a Pakistan and
Afghanistan correspondent for AFP ahead of the election from 2014 until
2017. However, due to the Pakistani military's focus on smothering online
dissent, bloggers and influencers who took to Twitter to express views that the
military did not like were arbitrarily detained by the security services.

'The purpose of this was to silence messaging that was critical towards the
army, which has ruled Pakistan for about half its existence and still continues
to be the primary power despite the ostensible latest return of democracy in
2008,' says Ahmed. 'The secondary purpose was to limit criticism of the army's
favoured party, the PTI of Imran Khan, who went on to win.'

Ahmed believes the military's silencing of influencers was 'extremely
successful', as its most vocal critics have since gone quiet. Those who were
targeted include journalist Taha Siddiqui, who now lives in exile in France, and
human rights activist and reporter Gul Bukhari – Ahmed's aunt – who was
briefly abducted by soldiers in June 2018. 'There is still some resistance but for
the most part dissent has been cowed and social media is now more or less
under control,' says Ahmed.

Although politics, culture and current affairs are the lifeblood of Twitter,
these are not the only spaces in which the platform's influencers have an

opportunity to change or have an impact on established narratives. Brands can also find themselves at the centre of a digital call-out storm if they release a campaign that is seen as offensive or out of step with modern points of view. Take beauty startup Uspaah, which got the wrong kind of attention in 2017 for its London Underground creative, encouraging men who had been neglecting their partners to buy them manicures and pedicures. This was shared widely on Twitter and deemed sexist. Brands judged to be pushing an aesthetic ideal on women have experienced a major backlash from their target markets ever since the appetite for millennial feminist commentary gathered pace in 2014. This was popularized by media companies aimed at this demographic, such as Refinery29 and the now-closed The Debrief, as well as blogs such as Vagenda.

Meanwhile, since 2018, actor and activist Jameela Jamil has made it part of her digital purpose to call out companies targeting young women with weight-loss products and the celebrities being paid to promote them.

Poorna Bell – a journalist, author and mental health influencer who frequently starts conversations about body positivity and representation on social media – believes Twitter has been a 'massive help' when it comes to telling brands they've got their messaging wrong. This is particularly important when it concerns standing up to a brand that suggests there is a right way to look, she adds. 'It means power is not wielded in the ivory towers as it once was, and brands cannot get away with lazy messaging that feeds into the harmful ideas we have been fed around our bodies,' she says.

Bell also thinks Twitter provides people with a counterweight to Instagram, where – thanks to image filtering, editing and perfection-focused narratives – one can get sucked into the 'compare and despair' cycle defined by the Royal Society for Public Health in Chapter 1 of this book. Prior to giving her 'following' list on Instagram a spring clean, she admits she spent months 'self-flagellating' if she found her appearance or dedication to exercising lacking in comparison to other users'. She says: 'Twitter offers a conversation around that and, to be honest, has educated and course-corrected me about things I took for granted, or wrongly assumed.'

Although the platform gives influencers the opportunity to address brands directly and publicly when their messaging is culturally out of step – making it more important than ever to sense-check campaigns – it doesn't always create a ripple effect of change. Plus-size fashion blogger Chloe Elliott frequently uses Twitter to call out retailers for their designs aimed at this consumer and for the fact many do not cater for this shopper at all. However, she admits many more ignore her tweets despite the traction they get from her community. 'They care so little about their plus customer that they don't take the time to respond to us,' she says. Those who do engage often say they are working towards representation, but Elliott highlights this has been their answer for so long that she no longer feels reassured by it and is perplexed by many fashion brands' seeming unwillingness to produce plus ranges or feature them in marketing campaigns. She highlights: 'The more brands do this, the more they alienate us and therefore the less likely we are to continue to shop with them.'

Impact on the media authority

The rise of Twitter as a crowdsourced news outlet has without doubt resulted in a closer relationship between traditional media and consumers, but has also somewhat eroded the authority of the former, primarily because it allows individuals with unknown agendas – and seemingly no agenda – to have the same level of perceived jurisdiction as an entire news organization.

Wendling explains:

Social media has, in effect, flattened authority. If someone has 100K followers and a local newspaper has 100K followers, these two things are seen as being the same. There are people on there who are very extreme and have huge follower counts. It's worth remembering that this is all built in to Twitter and the result of conscious decisions about design made by a few individuals who created this world.

He adds: 'The follower count could be much less prominent.'

Wendling also believes the unclear way in which the platform distributes verification – the blue tick which suggests legitimacy – is also problematic, as it leaves users with no sense of why one should trust this account more than another. Twitter states the blue tick indicates to users that 'an account of public interest is authentic', although it also argues verification does not signal endorsement.

Despite this, Wendling argues a deeper understanding of why people are verified would be helpful, as this symbol is widely seen as a hallmark. 'There are people who are verified on Twitter and they talk absolute garbage', he says. 'Verification is given out in such a flat way – it's not just for organizations or news organizations. There is no real clarity on how they do this.'

The fact that a media organization and an individual could both have the same number of followers and both be verified by the platform is problematic for news media, as it suggests they hold equal weight. This is then compounded by the noise and hype of continuous tweets which can seem to make the fundamentals of any news story straightforward and quickly understood, when actually the facts have yet to become clear. Rifkind admits it is 'so easy to get the wrong end of the stick'. He says: 'Every election, I'm sent to a different part of the country to talk to people and the last time it was Cornwall. I would have got a completely different idea of what people thought if I had been sitting at my desk looking at Twitter.'

Rifkind also cites Western perception of the Arab Spring – a series of uprisings in the Middle East, which started in 2010 and led to the fall of leaders in Tunisia, Egypt and Libya – being driven by commentary on Twitter, which did not provide an accurate representation of what was actually going on. He admits: 'A lot of Western journalists confused what people were saying on Twitter with what people actually thought.'

Ahmed, who is now reporting from Washington, agrees the platform can be 'inflammatory', given the drama of the Trump presidency, but argues that, pre-Twitter, people who were obsessed with Beltway politics simply channelled this into cable news. Twitter has made everything more accessible and interactive – which one could conclude has been a positive impact – but it has also made it easier to mislead not just the public but the media too.

A prime example of this is the coverage of the apparent incident between the 'Covington teens' – a group of boys wearing 'Make America Great Again' hats – and Native American Nathan Phillips at an anti-abortion March for Life rally in Washington in January 2019. A clip which went viral on Twitter appears to show one of the boys blocking Phillips – who is also a military veteran – and silently mocking him while he chants and drums.

The seeming disrespect of this action resulted in a flurry of comment pieces and outraged tweets. However, a longer video released after this showed Phillips had approached the teens first, placing himself in between them and another group – the Black Hebrew Israelites. He later said he did this to diffuse tension between the two. Rather than mocking him, it is possible the Covington teens are simply not sure what to do, and actually some join in with his chanting.

Ahmed says:

The way that story was reported by all major media outlets turned out to be ultimately quite unfair to the teenagers. The reason for that is the speed at which the news cycle is now driven by social media, together with a tendency by outlets to assume that because something appears to fit a broader narrative – in this case, racism in the Trump era – it must be the case.

He admits the consequence of this is less due diligence and a resulting situation where 'a lot of people can have egg on their faces'. He adds: 'I think we're still figuring this out and certain salient lessons will come along the way that will hopefully cause us to reflect and correct our approaches.'

On the flipside of this is BAFTA-award winning journalist Mark Daly, who does not report on news as a result of virality or noise on Twitter, but does create a large amount of discussion with his documentaries, which have most prominently covered racism in the UK police, the 1993 murder of London teenager Stephen Lawrence and issues within Scotland's 'Old Firm' football clubs, Celtic and Rangers. As a result of Twitter, he is accessible to viewers, making their experience of his work an interactive one in which he may enter into a debate if someone puts forward valid criticism. 'I don't engage with everybody but if someone's got genuine beef with your journalism, I think it's important to respond,' he says, adding, 'I've had thousands of people jump down my throat only to find they haven't actually watched the documentary.'

Aside from his personal use of the platform, he believes Twitter has been a positive thing for the media as it gives viewers an 'immediate route' into a story. He also acknowledges that traditional media must integrate social platforms into its output if it is to survive in the face of digital. 'Not everyone has time to sit down and watch your documentary or read your feature,' he says. 'Audiences for the programmes I make are shrinking and you need to find ways to get people engaged.'

However, he does make an interesting point about how Twitter has been to the detriment of traditional media, in that – in an age where journalists are encouraged to double up as commentators on Twitter – finding someone with a small enough digital footprint to go undercover is extremely difficult. Although he had been working as a newspaper journalist for five years in Scotland before he joined the BBC to personally go undercover as a police trainee for his 2003 BAFTA award-winning documentary *The Secret Policeman*, the publications he had written for did not have a big enough digital presence for this to prohibit him. He says he was able to do the job as a 'clean skin' – someone with no links to journalism.

'From a deep cover point of view, that's completely impossible now for anyone who has a presence on social media because people will check Twitter and Facebook,' he says. 'Getting an operative for undercover is more difficult for sure – it helps if they have journalistic experience and no social media presence. You can work with someone who has no links to journalism but that brings its own problems.'

In other words, in attempting to keep up with the second-by-second flow of information and daily minutiae coming from all angles on Twitter, traditional media is potentially blocking itself from getting to the root of the larger issues that underpin society, often away from the internet, and should be interrogated.

Also posing problems to media authority is the vast number of opinion pieces being defined as journalism and circulating on the platform. Wendling says: 'There are a lot of people calling themselves journalists when they are actually commentators.' The line between news and comment has certainly been blurred in the race to generate engagement, audience growth and achieve the loudest voice on Twitter. In addition, the platform's significant ability to define the news agenda based on tweets and issues that gather traction due to user behaviour continues to challenge mainstream media's own agenda and, in many cases, define it. Influencers on Twitter may be somewhat stuck in a bubble until an editor or producer offers them a route to a mainstream audience, but it is the numerical information related to their commentary – the likes and retweets – which result in this powerful springboard.

Rifkind believes the ongoing democratization of the news via Twitter and influencers means the future of mainstream media online is paywalls, citing the proliferation of fake news as a major catalyst for consumers to invest in trusted sources. 'There's so much rubbish out there,' he says. Ahmed agrees that ultimately a desire for truth will perpetuate the need for traditional media in the noisy digital landscape. He says: 'We still need communicators who can distil the raw information, contextualize it, and, of course, in the era of booming misinformation, fact-check it.'

In conclusion? Twitter and the influencers driving its conversations are unlikely to replace or cancel out traditional media companies, but Twitter is problematic in that its ability to define what is important and who is authoritative can be misleading. The future of information is a combination of all three sources, but journalists will have to fight harder than ever to be heard and to counter the platform's dominant driver – base emotion – with fact.

WE ALL LIVE IN A CHEESE SUBMARINE

IT WAS DECEMBER 2018 AND *The Times* columnist Hugo Rifkind had decided to post a thread on Twitter explaining Brexit via an analogy in which he compared the UK leaving the European Union to building a cheese submarine.

In an article two weeks later, in which he explained his decision, he wrote: 'There I sat on my stairs, scrolling through Twitter and getting annoyed, which is basically my only hobby. The Brexit debate, I found myself thinking, was going through an even more glaringly dishonest phase than normal. So, as much for my own benefit as anybody else's, I had a crack at transposing its peculiar shape on to something else.'

That something else was a cheese submarine. Why? 'It was the most impractical thing I could think of that wasn't actually impossible,' he says.

Not everybody got that. One of the first replies I had back was somebody saying, 'Is it your contention that leaving the EU is impossible?' To which I could only reply, 'Is it your contention that building a submarine out of cheese is impossible?' Because the whole point was that it isn't. It's just very, very stupid and bound to not work very well.

The premise of the thread is that building a cheese submarine is madness, would never work and then UK Prime Minister Theresa May knew it wouldn't work. However, to gain and maintain power she had to pretend it would, and therefore proceeded, while her peers argued they could have built a better cheese submarine. Everyone is lying, proposes Rifkind, because it would be impossible to build a good submarine using cheese.

The thread went viral and received international news coverage, not just because it was funny but – according to Rifkind – because 'it explained Brexit to people who don't understand Brexit'. The analogy was also adopted by Harvard University government professor Yascha Mounk to communicate why the outcome of the UK's 2016 referendum was a 'predictable mess' and delighted users on Reddit.

However, possibly the most influential place the thread ended up landing? 'A German MP read it out in the Bundestag,' says Rifkind. 'Nobody laughed.'

THREE EXTRAORDINARY MOMENTS ON TWITTER

#SaveRahaf: Rahaf Mohammed was eighteen years old when she renounced Islam and fled her family in Kuwait hoping to reach Australia in January 2019. However, when her passport was confiscated in Bangkok, she barricaded herself into an airport hotel room and asked Twitter for help, documenting her experience on the advice of organization Human Rights Watch, who told her – no matter what – to keep possession of her phone. She told the world she was afraid that if she returned to Kuwait, her family would kill her. Within five days – in which her tweets were continually retweeted – Rahaf had been given refugee status by the UN and granted asylum in Canada.

#MeToo: The current incarnation of this movement began when actor Alyssa Milano posted on Twitter in October 2017: 'If you've been sexually harassed or assaulted write "me too" as a reply to this tweet.' The result? Thousands of women using #MeToo to tell their stories of sexual abuse and violence. The idea had come from a friend who – in the wake of the widespread harassment allegations made against Harvey Weinstein – suggested sharing the tweet to help everyone understand the magnitude of what women across various industries have dealt with. Milano went to bed directly after publishing the tweet and when she woke up, it had 55,000 replies. However, this wasn't the start of the #MeToo movement – it was founded, pre-hashtag, on Myspace in 2006 by activist Tarana Burke.

#EdBallsDay: This tradition began in 2011 on 28 April when the then Shadow Chancellor of the Exchequer for the UK and former Labour Party MP tweeted his own name. He claims he had intended to search for an article about himself on the platform at the suggestion of an aide, but he mixed up the search bar and the dialogue box. The result? Every year on 28 April, numerous people tweet two words in memory of the occasion: Ed Balls.

KEY TAKEAWAYS

- Twitter is driven by cultural moments and the political climate, meaning that for brands to use it effectively their social media manager must have the freedom to tap into the daily zeitgeist. Much of the content shared on the platform that is successful – meaning it gets retweeted a lot – is humorous shorthand, either referring to something current or using something current to refer to something relatable.
- Although meme culture is an enormous part of Twitter – and arguably the best place to share a meme if you want it to go viral – consider if this truly fits with your brand before attempting to break into this sphere. Prolific meme-maker Mollie Goodfellow highlights that if a company is continually engaging with a youth audience in their language on issues which affect them, sharing memes will feel like a natural addition to its publishing output. However, if a brand is aimed at an older audience more accustomed to using Twitter as a customer service tool, consider what value it brings to your consumer.
- Responding to influencers who call out brands on Twitter is crucial for companies that have either made a misstep with messaging or are not catering well to a particular bracket of consumers. However, avoid stock answers as there has been a realization – particularly among high-profile influencers – that while brands may promise change, from their perspective things stay the same. Consider sharing regular updates about ongoing solutions for ongoing developments to avoid falling victim to Twitter's call-out culture.
- Key influencers on Twitter are not using the platform to promote products or brand deals but to get the attention of producers and editors at traditional media brands in order to springboard their ideas to a mainstream audience. For them, this is where the true value lies, as even those with hundreds of thousands of followers cannot necessarily change their point of view or engage them to act upon something. The phrase 'preaching to the converted' has been used repeatedly.
- Although Twitter is most often cited in commentary about social media being used as a tool of the alt-right, this movement is actually using the platform in the same way as key influencers – to share ideas, news and 'pranks', which will grab the attention and coverage of the mainstream media. The online groups that define themselves by this ideology are mobilizing in other parts of the internet.

6

Instagram and a very millennial rebellion

Instagram offered a significant opportunity to millennials – and those of a millennial mindset – from 2014 onwards, in a depressing economic landscape that had been savaged by the global recession.

Even before Simon Sinek branded this demographic as entitled and lacking confidence in 2016, and Australian millionaire Tim Gurner opined, a year later, that the reason that they couldn't afford houses was due to regularly buying avocado on toast, there was a significant amount of mainstream media hostility towards this generation. They were 'snowflakes', uncommitted and difficult to manage. They were obsessed with the internet. Much to the frustration of older generations, millennials wouldn't toe the line.

As early as 2014 – which, coincidentally, is when Instagram began to boom as a space for fashion, beauty and lifestyle influencers who were keen to build a new kind of career – studies showed this group felt little affinity to many of society's institutions, not just the traditional workplace.

A report by Pew Research Center that year, called *Millennials in Adulthood*, found this demographic were less likely to get involved in organized politics and religion, carried significant levels of debt and were relatively unconcerned about getting married. Rather than engage with the reality of a stagnant job market and rising house prices, they turned their attention to an area of growth – digital and social media.

Another interesting point uncovered by Pew's work was that millennials, at this point, were a fundamentally positive generation. They did not want to get bogged down in the seemingly dire situation they faced after leaving school and university; they wanted to explore new spaces into which they could channel this positive mental attitude. After all, 2014 was economically defined by the threat of deflation and fears that the advanced world could fall back into recession in 2015. Did the traditional workplace offer the same security as it once did? Absolutely not.

However, most interestingly, this study found that, unlike older generations, millennials put themselves at the centre of their social media accounts. While others shared outward-looking content, they posted selfies and personal updates. Their immediate instinct when it came to defining what social media was for was to document themselves, hence why Instagram has been dominated by personal stories up until this point (in 2019, 90 per cent of the platform's users were under the age of thirty-five).

Instagram seemed to rebel against everything millennials were being told about the world they lived in. Mainstream media may have been saying that they had poor prospects, but Instagram suggested life could be fulfilling and beautiful. Lifestyle magazine brands continued to produce shoots focusing primarily on expensive luxury brands that millennials could not afford, while influencers produced fast fashion edits and hauls of cheap products. One mustn't underestimate how crucial the flooding of fast products into the lifestyle market in 2014 was when it came to defining many influencers' purpose. They became the shopping editors that millennials needed in order to make informed consumer decisions, trawling through endless drops of new low-cost garments and brands and discerning which ones were actually worth spending money on. Yes, a search on ASOS for a stripy jumper might surface hundreds of results, but an influencer could tell their followers which one, out of all of them, they should buy. And, unsurprisingly, 2014 was a golden year for fast retailers: Primark reported a 30 per cent profits surge and Boohoo announced a sales jump of 62 per cent. ASOS bucked the trend as its share price dropped by 31 per cent due to startup costs of entering China, but still expected to make profits of £45m that year.

Meanwhile, millennial-focused startup digital media brands such as Refinery29 and Buzzfeed started to ape influencer content formats, having recognized that their target market most desired that particular style of editorial. While traditional lifestyle media continued to prioritize the overarching brand they worked under with one tone of voice and perspective, these new fast-moving publishers pushed diverse individuals to the forefront. Effectively, they shaped the brand and the business followed, rather than the brand being a singular, unmoving philosophy.

Despite the fact that millennials tapped into a rapidly growing new sector of entertainment through Instagram as the world around them stagnated, much like YouTubers before them, their decision to tune in was depicted as dropping out. However, beyond data about the economy and surveys bullet-pointing millennial behaviour, ask any influencer about life pre-Instagram and there is a unanimous dissatisfaction with the other options that were available to them. Unlike the early YouTuber mentality – which was gung-ho and adrenaline-fuelled – the Instagrammer mindset was simply that they had nothing to lose.

Photographer Jonathan Daniel Pryce – also known as Garcon Jon – was established on the platform by 2014, having joined in 2012, and admits the job market for a millennial, post-graduation, was not encouraging. Speaking about the economic climate when he got his marketing degree from the University of Strathclyde in 2009, in comparison to when he started studying in 2005, he says: 'When I went to university, we were told how beneficial it would be after graduation if you got a first class degree. Then the recession happened. I got a first, and no one cared – but I was aware of how social media was changing the world of work.'

For fashion blogger and author Katherine Ormerod, it was experiencing how limiting a traditional full-time job was for an influencer who had built an audience that spurred her to reconsider how her career might progress. Having grown her Instagram as an editor at *Grazia* magazine, she describes how capitalizing on this achievement became problematic. 'Brands would ask me to work on things but back then no one was allowed to do anything like that,' she says. 'I couldn't build out my career because of my contract.'

For Sheri Scott – entrepreneur, and founder of blog Forever Yours, Betty – her realization that Instagram was a route to building an independent business came after two experiences in the traditional job market left her feeling underappreciated, uninspired and burned out.

The first was managing a popular vintage luxury concession in a well-known department store in Glasgow. 'I was size 0 and getting paid £13K a year for 60 hours a week,' she says. 'Management wouldn't give me a pay rise and after three years in the job, I knew I couldn't do this forever.'

A pit stop in a better-paid position made it clear to her job satisfaction was the key to contentment. 'I'd overestimated how much happiness money would bring me and, to be honest, I had nothing to lose.' Using Instagram and her blog as springboards, she applied her skills and contacts to her own personal brand, proving she was a hard-working, reliable and creative resource for companies keen to improve their digital presence. These days, Scott's blog and popular Instagram are the smallest parts of her business empire, which includes brand consultancy and a modern greasy spoon cafe called Roll with It.

This desire to build something through which part of the return was contentment feeds back to the findings of Pew Research Center that millennials are a fundamentally optimistic generation. However, traditional options available to them at this point did not nurture that characteristic and, using Instagram as a tool, they decided to forge a new path. Rather than being steeped in economic gloom and doom, this was centred on creating editorial in a fresh way on a platform that their generation adored.

Ormerod says: 'At that point it seemed like you had two choices: do something really unfulfilling for lots of money or something really fulfilling for no money. I just couldn't find a balance when I was working for other people and you had to choose one or the other on the traditional job market.' So Ormerod – and many others like her – rejected both options and embarked on a new career path that was, in its essence, a very millennial rebellion.

The early-adopter trajectory

Photographer Finn Beales joined Instagram at 10.47 pm on 11 November 2010. To give the extent of his early-adoption context, the platform had gone live on 6 October that same year and, thanks to running a web agency, he had heard about the app through the media grapevine. Back then, an Instagram community was yet to emerge but its functionality was useful for altering images. 'I thought it was more of a Hipstamatic photography app for filtering,' he says.

Beales uploaded a picture and then didn't open Instagram again for approximately one year, until a colleague announced he was switching from BlackBerry to iPhone – just so he could use the platform. Motivated by the strong desire of his peer, the photographer read up on how to use it and started sharing his work. By that point, it had developed into a community for creatives. 'It was very collaborative and positive and not corrupted by money or this concept of influence,' he says. 'It was about engaging with that community because you liked being part of it.'

Also there in the early days was Ramona Jones, founder of blog Monalogue, who – like Beales' colleague – had got an iPhone specifically so that she could join Instagram. 'I'd saved up my pocket money,' she says, describing the app as being very 'hipster'.

'Initially it was very much about composition and you had to shoot on your camera phone,' she says. 'It was quite repetitive – I remember a lot of grungy pictures of cityscapes.'

Photographer Jonathan Daniel Pryce joined in 2012 and recalls specific content formats becoming popular on the platform due to technology restrictions of the time. 'It was all about taking flatlays of your breakfast or long roads, because symmetry was very popular,' he says. 'As the technology got better, it became more and more possible to take pictures that looked good on a small screen.'

Jennifer Dickinson, digital editorial director of NET-A-PORTER, joined in early 2011 and – like Beales – admits nobody could have predicted at that point how powerful the platform would become. 'I don't think people really knew what they were doing with it,' she says. 'I remember a designer I followed posted a picture of his boyfriend's penis covered in daisies and I'm pretty sure he didn't think it was public. We just didn't really know what it was.'

She also recalls that images that were geometric and dominated by 'neatness' were more popular than anything else. 'I was working at *Harper's Bazaar* at that time and posting the latest cover of the magazine on my desk styled with sunglasses or something like that,' she says. 'Those pictures did better than anything else.'

Audience growth in that first era – from 2010 to 2014 – was, according to early adopters, extremely straightforward. If a user got more than a certain number of likes, their content would automatically be promoted in the 'Explore' section of the platform and, even at its height during that period, users peaked at 300 million. Competition wasn't sparse but the app was a much cosier place to be.

Alongside this, being featured as a suggested user or on Instagram's blog – as both Jones and Beales were – led to enormous spikes in audience numbers. The former remembers being sent cards from the company and having the sense it was entirely community-focused, while the latter wrote photography tutorials for the company, which accelerated his growth significantly. 'There were only about six people working for Instagram at that point,' he says. 'I would email Kevin Systrom directly.'

However, less competition and more recognition from the platform itself were not the only ways in which users gathered followers in the first era of Instagram. Experimenting with content formats, before obsession with engagement and gaming the algorithm were commonplace, allowed creators to hit their stride with less anxiety about popularity and a greater focus on interests – figuring out what exactly they wanted to use it for.

Calgary Avansino – ex-*Vogue* editor turned influencer turned entrepreneur – began using the platform to document her travels and imagery from the front row of fashion weeks in 2011, but never posted pictures of herself or shared captions. 'My ah-ha moment occurred when I started talking about what I ate, how I cooked and encouraging others to make changes,' she says.

For Pryce, it was a specific project that resulted in soaring follower numbers: 100 beards, 100 days. 'This basically meant I posted a picture of a bearded guy everyday', he says. 'It was such Instagram-friendly content at the time and within four months I had ten thousand followers. My audience has never grown as fast since that project'.

Although success on the platform was more possible in its first three years, it was far from guaranteed. For many who had established themselves on other social networks, creating desired content and a community eluded them on Instagram and, in some cases, that continues even now.

Dickinson says: 'You were expecting to see all the people who were influencers on Twitter have the same success on Instagram, but for some reason many just didn't cross over. What they were doing didn't work on both platforms, and this allowed new people to come through.'

The 2014–15 lifestyle boom

Although the fashion industry started to really see the potential of Instagram in 2013, the influencer boom didn't come along until the following year, when people started to feel left out if they weren't using it. The company had spent four years going from zero to 300 million users – not to mention adding Android users to the mix in 2012 – and from 2014 proceeded to add 100 million users a year until 2017. As of 2018, it was able to report one billion users.

At this point, the platform witnessed the explosion of lifestyle-focused accounts, led by beauty, fashion, food and parenting influencers. While the original community – focused on creativity and photography – continued to flourish, this was the content that turned Instagram from a quirky, fun app into a force to be reckoned with. Suddenly, aesthetic was no longer the domain of the authoritative media and brands. If Twitter democratized the written word, Instagram democratized the human image.

For Kat Farmer, founder of fashion blog Does My Bum Look 40 in This? and a former headhunter, creating fashion content was a rebellion against archaic style rules about what women of a certain age should wear. 'It was putting two fingers up to the old adage that you need to be careful about looking like mutton,' she says. Talking about why her approach has struck a chord with so many women and led to a highly engaged Instagram audience, she adds: 'I like to think I've found a style that straddles that precarious line between mutton and tramp which is wearable every day.'

Her main aim was to 'challenge preconceptions' and, since doing so, she believes a wider change has occurred in terms of what is expected from her age group. Personal style, she says, is lifestyle- rather than age-related. 'I remember when people balked at wearing a maxi dress on the school run, whereas now it's definitely the norm.'

Plus-size fashion blogger Chloe Elliott – who started her website and joined Instagram in 2014 – states the platform has been 'absolutely vital' in pushing the importance of body diversity and positivity. 'I don't think there's another platform like it for sharing a message so widely,' she says. On the flipside, she points out that full representation – particularly in fashion retail – is a battle yet to be won. With her content, however, she has challenged stigmas and stereotypes through working with brands such as Nike and encouraging her followers to enjoy their bodies and fashion. As with Farmer, Instagram has been an opportunity to rebel against style rules created by an authoritative traditional media that did not engage with women who looked like her or did so in a negative way.

For Elle Ferguson, relatability and followers being able to re-create her look has always been crucial. She says: 'I feel there is an art in dressing for real life and I think that's what resonates with my audience.'

This narrative of applying fashion to the everyday and this being the power of the style influencer is a point that comes up again and again. Farmer believes the appeal of her look is the combination of 'classic basics with more on trend pieces that are accessible to everyone'. Journalist, author and fashion blogger Ormerod notes she could have just as easily been a luxury style influencer, but opted to cover a mix of high-end high street and luxury accessories because she wanted her followers to 'actually be able to wear the clothes'. Dickinson argues influencers working in this space are basically modern fashion editors. 'They are just styling edits of pieces on themselves.'

When it comes to interacting with her audience, Ferguson has taken an 'extremely transparent' approach, telling her followers when pieces were cheap and highlighting when she was saving up for more expensive items such as shoes and handbags. 'I think by being honest, it broke down the barriers and allowed my profile to become something that women were invested in,' she says. Showing their audiences things that aren't immediately attainable is a classic trait of early bloggers like Ferguson – a habit they picked up in the days before the industry was monetized. While some influencers who began their career on Instagram have never attempted to go deeper than the glossy images they post, early bloggers must hold on to some narrative of normalcy – even if their lives are fantastical – to maintain that connection with their long-term core audience.

Ferguson was also an early adopter of Instagram – ditching her BlackBerry for an iPhone when this was the only option if one wanted to use the app – and had nailed her style pre-2014 boom when it felt like there was room to be experimental. 'I think there was magic starting then because there was a naivety with what you were doing, there was no bar set so high that it was unattainable and nothing was "curated" on anyone's feed,' she says.

Influencers using Instagram to start the conversations they wanted to have and publish the content they wanted to see was also a trait of the parenting community, which collectively proved the idea of motherhood as a singular experience did not exist. From 2014, there were a plethora of narratives and aesthetics for consumers to choose from to tune in to – from perfection-focused influencers demonstrating a love-drunk idyll, to those covering the chaotic juggle of raising children and progressing careers.

Violet Gaynor, co-founder of cult parenting website The Glow, started producing content for this and its accompanying Instagram having realized there was no editorial – in print or online – that discussed transitioning from career to motherhood. 'How could that not exist?' she says. 'In that moment, I figured if no one is doing it yet then it's either the best idea or the worst idea – it was this light-bulb moment.'

At this point, she was an editor for *InStyle* magazine and noticed that although many of the women in fashion who were being profiled by lifestyle media were mothers, their children were conspicuously missing from the stories. 'They had kids at home and this was a huge part of their lives. I thought it had to be a bigger part of how they were being portrayed.' Thus The Glow was born – a combination of beautiful photography and honest stories about motherhood, shared by successful women with creative careers. Its initial aim? To help women who wanted to be able to envisage how they could do it too. Gaynor says: 'I always wanted to be a mom but I looked at my life and thought there was just no room. So many women go through that because you can't picture it until it's your reality.' This is a common goal of parenting influencers on Instagram – more times that not, their motivation for building communities is helping people navigate parenthood as much as it is sharing their own stories.

One influencer in this camp is Clemmie Telford – creative director and founder of website Mother of All Lists – who noticed Instagram would be an effective way for brands to reach fellow parents if they could do this empathetically. After an advertising agency gave her a brief in 2015, when she had just 500 followers, asking her to post content on her account in return for a fee, she realized 'something was going on'. 'It made complete sense,' she says. 'Brands were trying to talk to families but you only really understand what it's like to be a parent when you actually are a parent.'

A springboard for independent creatives

Elsewhere on the platform, a rising number of creatives were using Instagram to skyrocket their careers and create lucrative businesses through sharing their work and the processes behind it. Highly styled images accompanied long, detailed captions that aimed to show the labour and skill of the independent maker, and this combination attracted mass audiences who were passionate about these narratives of slower production. Creatives working in ceramics, textiles and woodwork have particularly engaged communities, which are often a combination of their peers and their customers. Meanwhile, short-form poetry has been popularized by writers who have shared verse on the platform which captures themes and feelings related to popular culture, taboo subjects and distinctly more inner monologues. Rupi Kaur posts couplets and quartets that succinctly tap into feminist and moral ideas, while Hollie McNish uses her poetry to cover the realities of sex, masturbation and periods, poetry that she frequently performs live. On the flip side of this, there are millennial poets whose work is so culturally relevant that Instagram users turn their verse into graphics for Instagram and these are shared prolifically. A good example of this is Warsan Shire's writing about refugees and forced migration, which she herself does not publish on the platform but others distribute across social media independently as it so encapsulates the compassionate mood felt by many about the refugee crisis.

Potter Jono Smart joined Instagram in 2015 on the advice of his sister and having seen counterparts in Brooklyn use it to springboard their profiles and businesses. 'There was definitely a way to make a living from it,' he says, noting the news feed was still ordered chronologically making fast growth infinitely more possible. Adopting the ecosystem method of acceleration popularized by YouTubers, Smart grouped together with other independent artists to share advice. 'There were ten or twelve of us growing at the same time.'

Over the next two years, his audience 'grew and grew' and he was able to sell directly to consumers rather than dealing with shops and galleries. He attributes this to regularly posting content and maintaining the human tone of voice he started with – as opposed to creating a brand voice – as demand for his work grew. He has also maintained a clean, minimal aesthetic throughout his feed. 'The pictures are about 70 per cent of what you're saying,' he says. 'Behind the scenes content does well, as does talking about your failures as much as your triumphs.'

For some creatives, Instagram has represented a chance to do something distinctly more political than simply build a brand, particularly since the US election of Donald Trump in 2016. One of these people is craftivist Shannon Downey. Better known as Badass Cross Stitch, Downey's furious embroidery piece, which read 'Boys will be ~~Boys~~ held accountable for their fucking actions', went viral on Instagram in the wake of the #MeToo movement in 2017, through which women shared their experiences of sexual harassment and abuse. This was catalysed by numerous actors' allegations of rape and inappropriate behaviour against Harvey Weinstein in the same year, led by actor Rose McGowan.

Describing how it felt to see her work go viral under the banner of such a cultural watershed moment, Downey says: 'To know that something I created, connected with so many people around the world, was astounding to me. And that so many folks used it as the illustration for sharing their #MeToo stories was incredibly powerful.' She adds: 'I had no idea that piece would take off like that.'

Downey actually created the embroidery in 2016 in a 'rage flurry' after a video in which Donald Trump tells US television presenter Billy Bush he felt able to grope women without their consent was published by *The Washington Post*. 'I thought for sure this was the nail in the coffin for him,' says Downey. 'The piece didn't actually go viral until Harvey Weinstein was outed. One can never predict these things, I guess.'

While segments of the fashion, lifestyle and parenting Instagram communities seem deeply conflicted by the direction in which Instagram, and some of the things they have experienced as influencers on the platform, happy endings – or continuings – seem to be much more prevalent than anxieties in the platform's creative communities. Smart says: 'Me and my partner are now both supported by our studio – almost everyone who buys our work comes via Instagram, it's our whole life.'

Meanwhile, so passionate are people about Downey's creative that a nameless group determined to protect the origins of her iconic cross-stitch now police the internet and call out any organization or individual using it without crediting her. 'They don't want me erased from this moment, as happens too often to artists these days, and for that I am deeply grateful,' she says.

The creative most concerned about how Instagram will develop and impact on industry is Beales, who is perhaps one of the very few users who can say they were there from the start. 'I see a lot of really bad work and that's what annoys me about the influencer industry,' he says. 'I love good advertising but that takes time – so much of what I see on Instagram is vacuous, cheap content.'

He is also dubious that so much focus on 'the self' can lead to happiness, describing the influencer industry as 'the very essence of the self'. However, he does concede that he is 'massively grateful' for the platform and will continue to use it. 'I only follow people whose work I love,' he says. 'I've become friends with them, travelled to meet them and we've collaborated. It's an incredible way to expand your network – perhaps I look at it this way because I grew up in a small community.'

What has the impact been and where is it going now?

With Instagram now being such a significant part of the consumer journey, it's no surprise that brands are zeroing in on how they can further leverage their businesses via the platform. In 2019, it introduced an in-app 'checkout' feature, allowing users to buy direct rather than go to brand websites, and providing this functionality seems to be a signifier that becoming the ultimate shopping destination could be its future. For some influencers, however, the ongoing commercialization of Instagram is increasingly a turn-off.

Entrepreneur, YouTuber and author Patricia Bright says: 'I love creating pictures and seeing people but it's becoming a walking advert with people just pushing more products.' Meanwhile, Ramona Jones says she already sees it as a shopping channel more than anything else, perhaps because consumers are being fed advertising – from both influencers and brands – at such a high frequency. Lifestyle blogger and journalist Esther Coren agrees: 'Absolutely everyone seems to be selling something.' Photographer Pryce thinks people accept this as the imagery being used is 'artistic' but highlights: 'It's exactly the same as a website spamming you.'

The power of influencers to promote and sell product successfully is evidenced in how much control they now have over campaigns. Pryce – who frequently shoots for fashion brands – says: 'They are given the choice of the photographer, director and most of the budget.'

In his opinion, this isn't always a good thing. 'Some brands will go for someone who is completely inconsistent with them because they seem popular and they think they have to work with influencers,' he says. 'In some cases, it would make much more sense to just work with a model, but audience and engagement numbers have become so important.'

The growth of Instagram from small community to noisy publishing platform filled with millions of destinations for beautiful imagery has undoubtedly had an impact on what it takes to get cut-through. No influencer wants their content to be passively scrolled past. Ferguson admits that while she would happily pose in front of a garage door in the early days, now she is 'scaling cliffs to get the shot'.

But some influencers refuse to be pulled by the tide towards more extreme creative to maintain the level of attention that was possible in the 2014 boom. Author, stylist and blogger Latonya Staubs says: 'It's so easy for people to be eaten alive by what things *seem* to be, or what they'd like to portray.' While she is invested in the conversations that happen on the platform and the business opportunities she has had as a result of it, she has no interest in keeping up with Instagram trends – something that influencers who are heavily focused on audience growth are fixated on.

Some influencers who are keen to innovate on the platform and steer away from the catch-all bracket of 'lifestyle' are moving towards more tightly focused flagship accounts, supplemented by secondary Instagram pages through which they cover one specific thing. YouTuber Lydia Millen has successfully created an interiors community through this strategy, in which she documents the ongoing decor project that is her country home. Meanwhile Joe Wicks was so invested in the weaning process of his daughter Indie, he launched an Instagram account dedicated to this alone. Fashion blogger and author Ormerod created a separate parenting account after having her son

Grey, out of sensitivity towards what her audience may and may not want to see. Having personally struggled to conceive, she wanted her documentation of motherhood to be an 'opt-in situation' for her followers. 'The twenty-three-year-old woman in Manchester following me for style content doesn't want to know about my pelvic floor exercises – she's there for the shoes and feminist conversation,' she says. In doing this, Ormerod has been able to ascertain clearly what each audience wants and keep engagement high on both accounts. Speaking about the followers on her parenting account, she says: 'It is so engaged that sometimes I can get 200 messages following a single post.'

So how should brands proceed?

In the fight to keep up with Instagram's content churn, quick and dirty campaigns have become the norm for brands that have masses of cheap products to shift. These have been facilitated by the online influencer marketplaces detailed in Chapter 3, or by blogger programmes in which large amounts of imagery can be generated for relatively small amounts of money or in return for gifted products. For influencers riding the wave of having moderately significant audience numbers, this can ensure steady cashflow. Meanwhile, for brands charged with publishing several times a day, it provides a bank of content featuring people to whom their target demographic can relate.

At the other end of the scale, there are marketers who want to reach influencers' audiences but push an aesthetic and tone of voice which is completely out of character for the latter's platforms. They may be willing to pay a premium for this, but the control required by the brand makes the whole process miserable, says Coren.

Influencers who are focused on the bigger picture of what they can achieve and are effectively building brands, might question how effective either process is for actually selling or getting attention on Instagram. Neither produce the standard of creative that could be achieved through a more collaborative approach. Many content creators interviewed advised that better relationships with fewer people who directly represented their values and aesthetic would be a better way to work, and welcomed by the influencers themselves.

'I'd put in the hours to find someone who was a genuinely natural fit and then sort of let them run with it,' says Coren.

Personal relationships are the best way to produce content everyone can take pride in, says Ormerod, and highlights that these can be achieved through simply inviting someone for lunch or coffee. 'Brands do need to budget for building those relationships but it's a good investment,' she says. 'I will always, always over-deliver for brands with which I have a good relationship.'

However, marketers should take note: in a digital landscape where influencers have the majority of the power share, the ability to command audiences larger than they can and create product lines that sell out in hours, what is possible may be about to change imminently. One manager of many prolific influencers revealed confidentially that the majority of their clients will no longer publish sponsored content on their Instagram grids. They view this space as sacred and highly curated, therefore the only option for brands is to work with them on 24-hour campaigns for Instagram Stories. They pointed out these individuals are delivering hundreds of thousands of views via content for this part of the platform, but it will be interesting to observe how much more protective those serious, brand-building influencers will become. This could potentially be the kind of behaviour that polarizes the influencer industry – while content-creating guns for hire will, for a price, continue promotion wherever is necessary, those who have multiple revenue streams will begin to tighten up which channels are on offer for commercial activity.

The way in which Instagram has empowered influencers and democratized entire industries as well as the media has been, in some cases, much to the dismay and anguish of those still working in more traditional spheres. They have disrupted and redesigned what is possible and – like YouTubers before them – done so without asking permission. Sally Singer – creative director of US *Vogue* – attacked fashion bloggers in 2016, saying they were 'heralding the death of style'. Meanwhile, poet Rebecca Watts penned her disdain for her peers who had gained their readerships via Instagram and 'the cult of the noble amateur' in *PN Review*, directly aiming her criticism at Rupi Kaur and Hollie McNish. There seems to be a friction over the fact that their value was accumulated via public popularity rather than being distributed by respected figureheads and established institutions. Those who are threatened by their work unanimously address this by attacking its value – it is not clever or stylish, and it is negatively impacting on that which is.

Louise Nichol, who was editor-in-chief of *Harper's Bazaar Arabia* until 2018, believes the views of some in traditional media are the result of not understanding the skillset that influencers bring to the table. She says: 'I might have a politics degree and a postgrad in journalism, but I couldn't do a beauty tutorial on YouTube if you paid me. And if I could, I might be enjoying a very different lifestyle. I think we have to start valuing these skills without snobbery.'

Meanwhile, there is also the question of how valuable it is to work with influencers on Instagram when they might drive awareness and the appearance of digital popularity but do not represent the customer of the brand. In March 2019, Dior was the subject of criticism in Dubai when it hosted a reshow of its spring/summer couture collection and invited influencers over actual couture customers from the region. Marriam Mossalli, founder of Saudi Arabia luxury communications agency Niche Arabia, published a lengthy note on Instagram to her own significant following calling the brand out on this. 'Dior's biggest mistake is discounting the numerous women who actually buy the brand: from self-made entrepreneurs to wealthy socialites, replacing them with celebrity influencers.' She adds: 'Nothing is wrong with also including them (aspiration needs to be accounted for) but considering them alone is a mistake.'

Although this friction tends to make mainstream news, it has no effect – at least as far as their audience is concerned – on the popularity or legitimacy of the content creators involved. The audiences' reasons for following them are personal; their engagement is based on a connection they have with them as individuals and only they will decide when a particular influencer is no longer relevant.

FIVE INFLUENCERS WHO HAVE SPRINGBOARDED FROM INSTAGRAM

Foster Huntington: the ex-Ralph Lauren designer who quit his job in New York to live in a van and, in the process, invented the hashtag and nomadic Insta-friendly, outdoors lifestyle #vanlife. He started using it as a humorous reference to Tupac's 'thug life', but instead of getting the joke, millennials wanted to live the dream. He has since written four books.

Mo Gilligan: known as Mo The Comedian online, Gilligan started sharing relatable – almost Vine-like – short clips of his comedy on Instagram when he was still working in retail for Levi's and performing on the stand-up circuit. When Drake referenced one of his most famous catchphrases ('Julie, bring me a coupla cans'), he crossed over to television and the rest is history.

Jessamyn Stanley: the wellness blogger, yoga teacher and body positivity advocate redefined what a yogi looks like when she started sharing pictures of her practice, as a plus-size woman of colour, on Instagram. Since then, she has written a book and become a global inspiration for, and symbol of, inclusivity.

Jeremy Jauncey: the CEO and founder of Beautiful Destinations, who turned travelling to incredible places into his job. He and his team create content and creative strategies focused on travel for brands, and on his personal Instagram he documents his journeys and experiences as a WWF ambassador.

Busy Philipps: as a television actress, Philipps had roles in *Freaks and Geeks*, *Cougar Town* and *Dawson's Creek*. However, it is her candid Instagram content documenting life as a mother-of-two – both on the grid and in Stories – which led to her landing a book deal and her own late-night talk show on E!, *Busy Tonight*.

A SINGLE ILLUSTRATION THAT CAPTURED A GLOBAL FEELING

SELF-TAUGHT ILLUSTRATOR RUBY JONES was at home in Wellington when news of the Christchurch mosque shootings – which killed fifty people and wounded fifty more, in her native New Zealand – broke on 15 March 2019. 'I was watching all of the events unfolding and I just felt overcome with emotion,' she says.' I could see everyone else in my social media feeds reacting the same, just in shock with no words like, could this seriously be happening here?'

Jones' response was to draw – something she did in the evenings and weekends alongside her full-time job in media – and the resulting illustration depicted two women hugging – one Muslim, and wearing a hijab – with the words 'this is your home and you should have been safe here' written below. It summed up the sorrow, solidarity and regret felt by many watching in disbelief as another brutal attack played out in real time across several platforms.

'I did the drawing initially, and then the words came a little bit afterwards,' Jones says. 'The words were me having the realization that many of the victims were probably going to be people who'd come to our country to seek a better life.'

Jones posted the picture on Instagram and that is when the message she wanted to share started to spread. Within forty-eight hours, her illustration had gone viral having been shared by celebrities such as Gigi Hadid, as well as by numerous people who simply felt it said everything they wanted to express. Within days, *Time* magazine had commissioned Jones to produce artwork to illustrate its coverage of the attack. Her response to the tragedy became a great number of people's response and in sharing one simple illustration, she allowed thousands of people to give the Muslim community one thing they might take comfort in: an apology.

'It has been so special how many people have connected with the image and obviously were able to find some tiny bit of light in it,' she says. 'I feel incredibly thankful for how much love it has received.'

KEY TAKEAWAYS

- Early adopters of Instagram were able to gather enormous audiences quickly due to less competition on the platform, a chronological algorithm and perks such as being featured on the company's blog or as one of its suggested users.
- Initial content formats that became popular on the platform – some of which are still prevalent now – are reflective of technology at the time. Smartphone cameras were able to capture neatness, symmetry and geometry better than anything else and therefore flatlays and cityscapes were the subjects of much of the photography.
- While early adopters joined Instagram to become part of its creative community, those who rose up in the 2014 boom wanted to share content that they felt was not being published by mainstream media or use the platform to promote an independent business.
- Brand-building influencers are unanimous in desiring more creative control when it comes to the messaging and aesthetic of sponsored content, to ensure it fits naturally within their feeds. Meanwhile, some of the most prominent ones who have multiple revenue streams are no longer publishing any commercial work permanently on their feeds, and instead are only offering opportunities on Instagram Stories.

7

Individualism and the niche community

It has become commonplace to attribute value to influencers based on the numerical success of their platforms – how large their audiences are and the amount of engagement they can generate from these via their content. As a result, working with those who have a mass audience in the first era of the influencer industry has been seen as necessary and desirable – the marker of a good campaign. And it certainly makes sense: the initial appeal of independent content creators was their ability to directly reach vast audiences thanks to their mass relatability, and the skilful way in which they didn't just represent themselves or a brand, but perhaps their whole generation.

However, as 'mass' became the dominant theme of influencer and digital culture, a counterculture of niche of communities and platforms emerged, driven by individuals who either wanted to use social media in a very specific way or did not feel represented by the narratives that should have resonated with them – demographically speaking – in mainstream media or by early-adopting mass influencers. This motivation to create something that either drew attention to a single issue or made space for previously taboo conversations to happen has in turn drawn very specific audiences to these niche communities. Rather than scrolling or watching passively, they identify passionately with the narratives and points being raised and feel a sense of belonging in these digital spaces, which previously was not the case. In addition, even though many of these influencers start from a place which is counterculture, their ideas tend to capture the zeitgeist of a certain group so succinctly that they experience fast growth. Their followers enjoy the feelings of discovery and ownership – they are not just part of an audience but of a movement – and the creators themselves have impressive cut-through due to bravely producing an aesthetic or tackling subjects which no one else has thought were important enough to cover with such a singular focus.

One person who understands what it's like to move against the tide is Devran Karaca, co-founder of Generation-Z entertainment network, Kyra TV. When he launched the company in 2017, most media companies were still creating content which would play into the Facebook video boom, but he was determined to develop and monetize a premium long-form proposition aimed at a youth audience.

'Everyone was talking a lot about shorter-form content,' he says. 'The gist was younger people didn't have the attention span for long form and, as a result, every video going out seemed to be no more than thirty seconds long. Meanwhile, we were looking at Netflix and Amazon, thinking how much they had redefined television and also concluding the idea that young people didn't want long-form entertainment was, in fact, bullshit.'

He also highlights the fact that YouTubers were capturing their audiences for hours every week. 'Younger generations want to interact with creators, get insight into their lives and feel closer to people. It definitely results in a more fanatical following.'

That's not to say Kyra immediately began releasing lengthy videos on YouTube – the team had to learn exactly what long form meant to its target audience and gradually build up a rapport with the people it was trying to reach. However, its ability to produce regular and consistent programming led to deep loyalty from its former flagship show, menswear series *PAQ*. Meet-ups with its four presenters in 2019 led to round-the-block queues of men and women desperate to talk to them about fashion and culture.

'Our videos began at six or seven minutes and now we're at twenty-five,' says Karaca. 'They drop at the same time every week and it's just like appointment to view, traditional television. Our audience always has that touchpoint.'

For Annabel Rivkin and Emilie McMeekan, founders of The Midult, a media startup aimed at 'grown-up women' that launched in 2016, a dissatisfaction with how their generation was portrayed by mainstream media resulted in them developing a counterproposal with their website, social media, podcast, book and events series. Frustrated by always being the target of think pieces and features about 'Agas and root touch-ups', they instead zoned in on anxiety, divorce and relationships to name just a few issues, approaching everything with humour and heart.

Rivkin says: 'We knew we were part of the healthiest, wealthiest, most dynamically connected generation of women in history and yet, in media terms, we felt that everything directed at us had been put through a strange and slightly sinister filter. As though they were talking to marketing men's *idea* of grown-up women.' She adds: 'Everyone seemed to be getting our values and hopes and anxieties wrong. Frankly, it felt lazy.'

The result is a hyper-engaged community which frequently expresses gratitude to the pair on Instagram for providing them with daily relief, and praises the accuracy in their depiction of this demographic. Although The Midult's core audience is its target thirty-five- to forty-five-year-old women, its fastest growing segment is their twenty-five- to thirty-five-year-old counterparts. 'Youth is glorious, but it doesn't have any wisdom,' says Rivkin. 'We are finding that younger women see us as a kind of emotional anchor.'

Going against the cultural grain was also at the heart of Olivia Purvis' decision in 2018 to launch her Instagram movement, The Insecure Girls' Club. At this point, narratives aimed at millennial women on the platform were still very much centred around 'slaying' – being a boss and, ultimately, giving the finger to anyone who got in their way. Early blogger Purvis was outgoing and confident generally, but also wanted to talk about her insecurities – the things that gave her pause, caused worry and made her feel vulnerable. The project was borne out of numerous conversations with friends, during which she recognized there was nowhere to continue and amplify these discussions online. She also had 'a real want to do something that focused on other women's stories'. She says: 'I've always interviewed women for my blog, and I almost wanted to create a community that could bring back the "social" side of social media and give women a space to talk about these things whereby they wouldn't feel embarrassed or worried about it.'

In addition to sharing the projects of other women that she finds empowering, revealing and relatable, Purvis interviews fellow creatives, freelancers and influencers about what makes them feel insecure. Issues that have come out of these videos include the meaning of work and the need for validation, as well as struggling with nerves when meeting new people.

For some niche influencers, the platforms they have created are less the result of a eureka moment and more down to the fact that it wouldn't have occurred to them to do it in any other way. Take Ben Hicks. His life's work is almost entirely dedicated to documenting nature, and in particular sea turtles, something which his social audiences on Facebook and Instagram are completely captivated by. Although he began his career shooting surfers all over the world, he became interested in the creatures after a marine biologist friend asked him to photograph them on her behalf, as he was experienced in working underwater.

However, he can trace why this felt like such a natural fit for him as a specialism all the way back to his childhood. This is also common among niche influencers – a deeply personal connection to their subject matter. He says: 'As a kid, I grew up near the ocean and spent my summers in North Michigan, where I'd see river turtles. Also, I had snakes, iguanas, dogs – all kinds of animals. I was always interested in nurturing and caring for animals. So, when sea turtles fell into my lap I thought: here is an animal that needs to be photographed and cared for.' Raising awareness of the precarious future facing almost every species of this creature is indeed necessary – the World Wildlife Fund has classified the animal as 'vulnerable' due to climate change, poaching and habitat destruction. He adds: 'They needed attention and I really enjoyed photographing them.'

Hicks is always looking for new digital platforms to promote his work and began using Instagram in 2012 but it was magazine *National Geographic* discovering his photography and sharing shots on its platforms in 2013 that significantly elevated his profile. 'That's when my work got international attention,' he says.

While Hicks has had a lifelong interest and love of animals, other niche influencers begin projects as a result of defining experiences. For Shannon Downey, founder of Badass Cross Stitch – a craftivism project focused on pushing topical views via embroidery – it was running a fast-paced digital marketing agency and desperately trying to find balance. She says: 'I was attached to a device 24/7 and I was burnt out.'

Cross-stitch became akin to meditation and the more she did it, the more deeply she began to think about issues around her. These thoughts would then manifest in her work and she started to see how an analogue art form could make a difference when it was at the heart of a digital – and offline – community. However, the project is rooted in her personal experiences which in turn have resonated with others.

'Gun violence was one of the first major craftivism projects I put out into the world,' she says. 'Living in Chicago, having a bullet come through my bedroom window while I was asleep and doing some work with young people who had been shot catalysed that project and exploration.'

Badass Cross Stitch has since been the subject of international news coverage thanks to Downey's seminal piece of work, 'Boys will be B̶o̶y̶s̶ held accountable for their fucking actions', being adopted by the feminist movements, Time's Up and Me Too. It went viral in 2017, as described in Chapter 6.

However, not every niche community is the result of a lifelong interest or desire to spearhead a counterculture movement. Some begin because the founders want to take normal issues regarded as small or unimportant and place them centre stage. This was the case with The Hotbed Collective. Co-founder Lisa Williams explains: 'Our niche is sex content for people who wouldn't define themselves as being interested in sex.'

Williams – along with co-founders Cherry Healey and Anniki Somerville – decided to corner this market after the latter two women started talking about long-term relationship sex at a Christmas party and, overhearing them, the rest of the room joined in one by one. Meanwhile, Williams – a journalist by trade – had begun blogging and found posts about sex after having children outperformed everything else by far.

The Hotbed now encompasses a chart-topping podcast, website, an Instagram community, a book and an event series, all focused on starting conversations about everyday sex. 'You know, the kind of sex that doesn't happen every day,' clarifies Williams. 'We realized that there was a lot of chat about dating sex and a lot about out-there sex, but not much about the kind of sex which happens when you've been together for a while, when there may be kids in the next room, or money worries, or body confidence issues you've never addressed.' Williams describes their approach as 'unashamedly vanilla' and driven by helping people 'who wouldn't normally prioritize pleasure to keep that little flame of passion burning bright'.

Digital identity: 'People don't believe in trends anymore'

Pre-social media, there was arguably a 'right' way to construct one's identity and there were media brands that broadly helped consumers navigate this. People could loosely nail their flag to the mast of specific magazines or newspapers that reflected how they wanted to live and dress, their political views and, in some cases, their ambitions. You may have bought *Vogue* not because you could afford the fashion in its pages but because the community it represented was one you most identified with and aspired to.

However, due to the rise of influencers and so many creators producing individualist content in the free-for-all digital landscape, many media brands of the pre-Instagram age now feel too rooted in a generic authority tied to one ideal of what style is to be deeply relevant to anyone. Indeed, a 2019 study commissioned by the Institute of Practitioners in Advertising (IPA), and carried out by market research company YouthSight, discovered the future of defining identity will be based on the unique taste of the individual rather than having the tone set by an external force such as a fashion media brand. A survey of 1,000 people aged between sixteen and twenty-three years old found that Generation Z care little about owning brands and numerical popularity on social media. In fact, the subject of social media drew a significant amount of disdain from the pool of interviewees. More than two-thirds did not believe in trends and only one in ten described themselves as trendsetters.

Jennifer Dickinson, digital editorial director of NET-A-PORTER, believes individualism in terms of identity has already happened and that it is a cross-generational phenomenon – the concept that there is a right or a wrong way to do fashion no longer exists. 'People don't believe in trends anymore, and embrace the opportunity to show their individuality so much more because they are seeing everything through the filter of individuals with whom they have chosen to engage on Instagram,' she says. 'We've lost the sense that there is one way to dress.'

Consumers can curate who they follow, and tailor their curation to their own individual beliefs, style and outlook. The rise of the niche influencer means there is a community in which everyone can find authentic peers and if this doesn't yet exist, then they have the tools to create it themselves. Ironically, that's not to say that this post-Instagram individualist approach has resulted in the death of homogeny, but nowadays homogeny has multitudes. In the same way that millions of people subscribe to a Kardashian aesthetic, there are also millions of people who would define themselves as minimalists, colour-focused, vintage enthusiasts or hypebeasts. These filter down into smaller, more niche communities but the point is that the concept of 'one size fits all' is completely dead.

Karaca realized this early on and as a result cast four individuals with very different, very distinct styles to present Kyra's menswear series *PAQ*: model Elias Riadi, musician Dexter Black, skater Danny Lomas and artist Shaquille Keith. In doing this, the show represented its target demographic – Generation Z, which has come of age in the era of the individual – more than a group of people who appear to subscribe to the same brand of lifestyle.

'I wanted to find individuals and put them at the forefront of our talent,' says Karaca. 'We found four guys who had very different senses of style but really good charisma with each other.' He adds: 'The audience crossover of the four guys' separate channels is actually quite low – each one has a very different energy and is a very different person.'

In keeping with the broad traits of Gen Z – who are, by all accounts, driven by shared issues more than anything else – the presenters were united by their positive approach and upbeat nature rather than by their look. This was also important to Karaca. 'I felt there were a lot of very negative voices in the market and we wanted to make this generation feel really good about themselves,' he says. 'Making people feel good is our mission and purpose.'

One influencer who has based her entire brand around an original perspective and aesthetic is Sheri Scott, entrepreneur and founder of blog Forever Yours, Betty. Her Instagram is dedicated to bright colours – at the centre of which is Sheri's orange hair – and narratives that reinforce a positive mental attitude. It is neither on- nor off-trend, but feels very much like it is the expression of her own unique brand. Although technically a millennial, she has taken a Gen Z approach to social media and decided from the start to publish content she thought was interesting, rather than playing to the crowd. 'If I did that, I'd just end up posting selfies all the time – they do get more engagement than pictures of anything else,' she says. 'But, to be honest, I'm not a numbers person, I'm not an analytics person and I think it would be boring if all you were doing was chasing likes.'

The realities of maintaining a niche community

Influencers who have built audiences in niche spaces not only become authorities but also attract a specific consumer who identifies tightly with their message. While a mass influencer may have a following that represents their general approach to a specific industry or culture, the niche influencer will never be to everyone's taste, but those who do appreciate them will engage continually with their narratives in a way that may be life-changing.

Hicks' focus on the environment, and threats to sea life from human behaviour, has resulted in his Instagram being a touch point for users who want to learn more quickly but do not have the resources. He says: 'There are people following me in developing countries, for example, who haven't been educated yet on the impact of single-use plastic and will message to ask why they shouldn't use straws. They want to know what the impact is. So, by sharing my story and putting my images out there, I can also help people.' Alongside this, he gives talks at schools and nature centres, having realized how important education is to his brand.

Also finding that helping people learn is a key part of his output is Ali Horne, a photographer, drone pilot and co-founder of adventure group The Highland Collective. A gang of young outdoors enthusiasts, they travel to the most remote, most beautiful parts of Scotland to spot wildlife, hike and gather content. They formed in 2016 to share what the country had to offer to tourists and where the best places to go for adventurers are. Combining a continual flow of information to their users, along with idyllic pictures from the wildest parts of Scotland, has resulted in a huge Instagram following and partnerships with high-end outdoors-focused brands. Speaking of the power the platform has had for the adventure community, Horne says: 'It's a great way to inspire people to make that extra effort to see new places and discover new cultures and views.'

Downey believes Badass Cross Stitch and the craftivism movement have ignited such a passion – and resulted in followers actually learning to embroider – because this allows them to communicate effectively and make statements that cut through the noise of social media. She says: 'I think it's the medium. It's unexpected and stops people in their tracks. I can say things through stitch – and be heard – that would be ignored if presented any other way. It's powerful.'

Meanwhile, Williams points out the only way to build a strong audience in a niche is to understand the nuanced reasons why your content resonates and repeatedly reinforce these through your messaging. Demonstrating this comprehension is crucial when it comes to maintaining their trust, she says, highlighting that The Hotbed Collective never approaches sex in a way that is intimidating. She explains: 'We know relationships and sex go on the backburner for our audience and so we never guilt-trip people into thinking they're not having enough sex or that they have to have athletic, performative or "event" sex.' She adds the audience relates most to content which focuses on trying manage a partner and a busy life successfully. 'One of our most-listened to podcast episodes is called "The Maintenance Shag", which is all about routine sex and the important role it plays in a relationship.'

A passionate audience driven by the same values as the influencer who views them as an authority is without doubt a key benefit of working with those who have built followings around a niche over those operating in a mass space. While the latter is creating something more akin to digital entertainment, the former has achieved authoritative influence. However, the flip side of this is monetization is a much more difficult task. Mass influencers working under the catch-all bracket of lifestyle could arguably be a good fit for a large number of brands but a niche influencer must adhere to a very specific narrative – one which may not provide a natural context for product promotion.

For example, journalist, mental health and body positivity influencer Poorna Bell launched her business FML (Fix My Life), which provides in-house workshops for brands on diversity, equality and mental well-being. However, she also produces a series of free events for young people trying to build careers in the media, as helping others – not selling things – is really at the crux of her brand.

Similarly, to spread the benefits of embroidery, Downey has taken a largely altruistic approach and, since 2018, has taught approximately 1,000 people to sew free of charge at community workshops. Her focus with Badass Cross Stitch is very much the wellness benefits it stands to offer people who get involved, and she is determined as many as possible will experience these. She says: 'I want everyone on the planet to learn how to embroider. I think it is a profoundly liberating medium. It's accessible, inexpensive, easy to learn, slows the brain down and has a deeply calming effect.'

Meanwhile, Hicks says he rarely produces sponsored content, adding: 'If I do, it is very much related to my purpose.' He regards this broadly to be photography and 'helping mother nature'.

For Rivkin and McMeekan, there is no question of them monetizing The Midult's website, newsletter or social media in conventional ways, as their primary aim was to develop a real connection with their audience and they believe commercializing content on these platforms would compromise this.

The former describes this strategy as a 'long, slow game' through which they have developed a consultancy arm that educates brands on how to communicate with The Midult demographic. Their consultancy is informed by data about what their audience responds to and through real-life learnings from their events, each of which includes a 'live therapy session' in which they 'drill into the rhythm of women's days, their preoccupations and desires'. Also, despite operating in a lifestyle space, the industries Rivkin is most interested in working with are financial services, property and automotive. 'They are just so ripe for reinvention,' she says.

To go niche in a digital landscape where success is defined by accumulating mass is a bold move but potentially may end up being the most effective way for influencers to build their brands moving forward as consumers identify themselves in a more individualistic way. Williams highlights that pinpointing that niche should be done via a thought process that involves considering whether or not you stand to make a real impact on a human-to-human level. 'It's like finding a gap in the market,' she says. 'It doesn't matter if it's a small gap, as long as some people need you, and if you're willing and able to meet that need, it makes sense.'

THE FIRST RULE OF GEOMETRY CLUB...

IMAGINE AN INSTAGRAM ACCOUNT ENTIRELY dedicated to one thing: black and white pictures of cool buildings taken from one very specific angle. Think this almost meta-approach to content for the platform could never work? Think again – tens of thousands of people have joined designer and photographer Dave Mullen's Insta-gang Geometry Club, for which, if you want to submit pictures and get them published, there are two rules to follow. First, the apex of the building you have photographed must be centrally aligned on both the X and Y axis and, second, the edges of the building's walls should fall off the image symmetrically at the same point. If you think that sounds a bit boring for a platform filled with imagery documenting incredible landscapes, food and fashion, there are many people who would disagree.

Started in November 2014 because Mullen liked the idea of a 'dedicated Instagram feed with strict limitations', Geometry Club was initially a personal project but it soon broadened out into a niche movement, driven by its community. Mullen wanted the page to include the world's best architecture but knew he couldn't do that by himself, so he decided to make it a collaborative effort. 'I built a website, published the guidelines and used Instagram to connect with people, invite them to join and contribute to the series,' he says.

The growth and unique proposition has resulted in equally unique experiences for Mullen. He says: 'The most memorable opportunity was to be invited to the Design Museum in London to explore and photograph its new building before it opened to the public,' he says. Another priceless experience was co-creating an iOS camera app just for people who are members of the club. 'We collaborated for a year on the project and released it for free.'

Although Geometry Club was a passion project that turned into a movement, it wasn't an overnight success nor was its growth either accidental or due to luck. Mullen says its growth correlates directly to the effort he has put into it through networking with fellow Instagrammers and messaging like-minded people he thought might want to contribute.

A year into the project, he began to contact design-focused magazines and blogs that he felt might be interested in the photography series and this led to coverage in *Creative Review*, *Swiss Miss* and *Aisle One* to name a few. 'I've spent countless evenings doing the groundwork to get the traction and attention that I think Geometry Club deserves,' he says. 'It was exciting enough to keep me motivated and eventually it paid off.'

THREE NICHE INSTAGRAM COMMUNITIES WITH INCREDIBLE TRACTION

Same Picture of Michael Cera: with tens of thousands of followers across Facebook and Instagram, this project is undeniably entertaining. Started by an anonymous user – who refers to their work as the 'Michael Cera Movement' – this is the 'Groundhog Day' of niche social projects in that it is literally the same picture of the actor posted repeatedly. Its genius? No matter what the captions say (sample: 'I love turtlenecks because whenever I shove my head through the opening of one I feel as though I have given birth to myself'), they always seem to fit well with the picture.

The Great Women Artists: started by art historian and curator Katy Hessel, this account features the work of a different female artist everyday – from graduates to classicists – and began while she was at university and writing a dissertation about abstract expressionist Alice Neel. As a result, Hessel realized how underrepresented women were in the industry. After graduating and visiting an art fair that only featured male artists, her mind was made up: she started the Instagram. This has led to speaking, exhibition curation and writing opportunities.

Plants on Pink: described as an 'online gallery' by founder Lotte van Baalen, this Instagram exhibits a very millennial-friendly curation of images focused on demonstrating the beauty of plants in front of pink backgrounds. Followers are invited to contribute their own images and the account has featured pictures from content creators from all over the world who are keen to share their compositions. Van Baalen also created the frequently used hashtag #plantsonpink to help spread the concept of her Instagram project.

SUCCESSFULLY GROWING ON A MORE NICHE PLATFORM

ALTHOUGH INFLUENCER AND BRAND FOCUS are most firmly on YouTube, Instagram and Twitter, the communities on smaller platforms such as Pinterest, Twitch and Snapchat are also led by influencers who shape the conversations and drive growth every day. One person who understands how to develop an audience and aesthetic to the benefit of her business is designer Nikki McWilliams, who founded her eponymous homeware and accessories brand in 2009. She was an early adopter of Pinterest, joining in 2011, a year after it launched, and since then has accumulated over one million followers on the platform. 'At that point you had to email the developers to request a login – as they weren't allowing people to sign up independently – so it was quite exciting to be granted access to such a promising platform at the time,' she remembers. Although she began using it to assist her personal projects, she realized as it developed that it was an efficient way to promote her business as well as the products she retailed online. 'I created a really rich variety of boards that encompassed everything from my inspirations, to meals and event planning,' she says. 'Soon after, my account was listed by Pinterest as a featured account, which helped me to grow my following.'

McWilliams – whose brand is inspired by pop culture and the idea of British tea-time – is known for her biscuit-themed cushions, which are featured on numerous boards across the platform, particularly those related to home renovation and interiors. She thinks the fact that users actively utilize Pinterest to plan 'big life events' is what makes the audience there different from that of equally visuals-focused Instagram. And, although she works primarily with brands on content for the latter platform, she wouldn't rule out exploring how she could monetize Pinterest too. 'I think the function to create collections of (other users') visuals on Pinterest gives it a totally different appeal to Instagram,' she says.

KEY TAKEAWAYS

- Niche communities online tend to be the projects of influencers who felt they were represented neither by their mass-targeting counterparts nor by mainstream media.
- These communities tend to be countercultural in either their narrative, aesthetics or formats and, from a business perspective, it is worth monitoring those that are fast growing in a niche while doing something unexpected. Consider Kyra TV founder Devran Karaca's decision to develop a long-form premium proposition at a time when his competitors were focused on shareable, quick-hitting snippets designed to go viral on Facebook. Following the gaze of individuals creating countercultural businesses is an effective way to potentially gain a glimpse into the future.
- Many niche-focused influencers have created their communities as a result of significant personal experiences; in talking about these experiences, their projects have an unshakeable authenticity. In addition, in sticking to a very tight narrative, all of those interviewed have been approached by traditional media brands, large movements and very specific kinds of brands whose values or aesthetic aligns tightly with theirs, meaning cross-promotion delivers their target audience rather than diluting their community as mainstream brands might.
- Monetizing niche communities poses a significant challenge to influencers who have built them, as they cannot stray from the values that have made them appealing to their core audience. Brands that are keen to work with this kind of influencer should consider proposing innovative partnerships involving events and other ways to help their followers, rather than presenting opportunities that involve sponsored content.

- The value in working with niche influencers is the highly nuanced understanding they have of their audiences, what they want and how to start conversations with them. They can tell brands not just what topics their followers might best respond to, but the subcategories within that which drive most engagement. As Williams highlighted with The Hotbed Collective, the audience is not interested in content about sex – they're interested in content about sex which leads to bigger discussions about managing life and how to fit sex into that.

8

A problematic industry

Logan Paul vlogging a hanging man in a Japanese forest famous for its frequency of suicide. Felix Kjellberg promoting a YouTube channel that produces anti-Semitic content. Jeffree Star's repeated use of racist language. Trolling, mob mentality, influencer fraud and burnout. The industry of digital influence is riddled with flaws due to the many egos and desires at play and the impression that fast money is available if one has a large audience and significant engagement. Brands want to sell products, managers are motivated by commodifying stories and influencers are addicted to immediate attention and fame. In their pursuit of getting what they want from audiences on social platforms, each party's behaviour has become more extreme and the problem is it's unclear who could police the influencer space. The knee-jerk response is that the technology companies should take responsibility but this would require a cross-platform treaty of no tolerance given it's rare influencers operate on only one. Then, there's the simple fact the social networks don't want to lose their most prolific – and often most controversial – content creators, some of whom have already claimed they are victims of censorship. After all, their ability to command audiences of millions is part of the commercial draw for brands to social platforms. Michael Wendling, broadcast journalist and author of *Alt-Right: From 4chan to the White House*, believes significant problems related to influencers and offensive content could be solved by legal changes. 'US lawmakers could say that social media companies are liable for the people on their platforms,' he says. 'It's not that far-fetched.'

However, the problematic nature of the digital influence industry goes deeper than trolling, intimidation and spreading vile points of view. For a start, there is the mental health of those creating content, many of whom are now stuck in an almost unmanageable cycle of daily supply and demand, in order to maintain high numbers of views and make enough YouTube advertising revenue to sustain their career. Despite being on a clear road to burnout – a YouTuber career-halter that has been on the rise since 2016 – they continue to prioritize the health of their audience's engagement over their own state of mind. Then, there is the proximity influencers have with their followers and subscribers, which – due to being set up like a friendship – can and has allowed influencers to exploit those around them, both their fellow content creators and their audiences. And what about influencer fraud – the practice whereby they have bought their followers and engagement from bot farms, and are selling brands access to an audience which has no real interest in them? On top of this, there are several significant moral issues about whether or not any of these issues matter to those financially fuelling the industry at all. In the race to achieve digital ROI, it seems the 'wild west' landscape of the industry is not just being determined by the influencers.

Death threats and hate-follows: welcome to the world of influencer trolling

Influencers with genuinely engaged audiences that operate as communities are major draws. However, the negative flipside of this is their followers believe that, as a result of them posting personal content – and often being paid to do so – they are fair game for trolling if they think they have done something wrong. Si Barbour-Brown – owner of influencer talent agency The Sharper

Group – admits the frequency and intensity of influencer abuse is 'definitely getting worse'. He says: 'The best thing the internet ever did was give everyone a voice and the worst thing the internet ever did was give everyone a voice.' The escalation of online conflict between influencers and their audiences appears to be accelerated by the fact that audiences transform from community to mob almost immediately, and that a mob grows quickly as trolls flock to their platforms. As discussion and sharing stories are group activities on social media, so too is attacking the people at the centre of the accounts they follow. For many influencers, trolling is a daily occurrence that requires no significant catalyst as their audiences are partially composed of 'hate-follows' – people who have subscribed to their content because they dislike them. Beauty blogger and Instagrammer Andreea Cristina Bolbea revealed in 2018 she had blocked at least 200,000 followers due to daily bullying, abusive messages and death threats.

Like Bolbea, mental health influencer and journalist Poorna Bell has taken to blocking people when she suspects they have bad intentions or if they upset her. 'I don't want their negative energy anywhere near me,' she says. 'My feed is my own, and people seem to think that – because it's public – I have to accept or put up with bad comments but I don't.'

While Barbour-Brown says the people who are guilty of trolling his clients are often children, it would be inaccurate to excuse this as an issue simply borne out of immaturity. Indeed, adults – even those with high profiles – are just as likely to get swept up in the frenzy of an influencer attack, as Scarlett Dixon, founder of blog Scarlett London, discovered when a staged sponsored Instagram post she published in 2018 was poorly received. The main criticism of the image was that it pushed a dishonest narrative – she was holding an empty mug and her breakfast 'pancakes' were actually tortilla wraps. In addition, on close inspection – facilitated by an online mob – her bedspread appeared to be printed with a large image of her. The combination of these things, added to the fact the post was an advert for mouthwash brand Listerine, resulted in a forty-eight-hour attack on Dixon which included death threats. In a post after the event, she revealed those sending her abusive messages included MPs, self-confessed feminists, popular actors and prolific journalists. She wrote: 'Each time I refresh my page, hundreds of new nasty messages pour onto my Instagram, Twitter and YouTube.' She added: 'There are now hundreds of thousands of tweets circling the internet, shaming me.'

Midwife and blogger Clemmie Hooper – known as Mother of Daughters on Instagram – was targeted by trolls via threads on Mumsnet and Instagram. She says: 'Sometimes the way people speak to you – you'd think you'd killed someone. People can be offended by absolutely nothing.' The lasting impact has been she now finds it difficult to post anything personal at all – despite her candid reportage of family life being the reason for her popularity – for fear of the reaction she will get. 'I've been trying to second guess people and by the time I write and publish a post, I just want to delete it.' Hooper also thinks people become fixated on the pursuit of 'having the last word'.

Journalist and blogger Esther Coren, who experienced trolling as a result of an article she wrote for Space NK about her daughter's lack of interest in her appearance, admits: 'It's incredibly frightening to be in the middle of a big online troll storm.' She adds: 'I don't want to sound dramatic, but I quite see how if you were young or vulnerable in some way you could, if the trolling was bad, consider suicide.'

Describing the sudden descent of an online mob as 'crazy', Coren admits she finds people's willingness to lash out on social networks difficult to understand. 'I would never, ever say anything to someone in an email or online that I wouldn't say to their face and even to someone's face I'd only ever be polite,' she says. 'It is not nice to see how otherwise sane humans can behave when they believe they are unaccountable.'

Many influencers think the option of online anonymity makes their followers feel they can launch vicious attacks without stopping to consider if they would behave in such a manner were they face-to-face.

There is also a sense of 'safety in numbers' upon which the mob thrives. This has allowed the more sinister marshalling of people who have digitally congregated under a shared political ideology and can be effectively deployed on a target who is depicted as representing everything the congregation is united against. This was the case with former Labour Party member and MP Luciana Berger who was the victim of an anti-Semitic campaign of abuse on Twitter in 2014 after the editor of neo-Nazi website The Daily Stormer rallied readers to harass her. An article by said editor Andrew Anglin gave readers advice on how to troll her and set up anonymous Twitter accounts in a way that made it difficult to trace the user. Wendling recalls: 'He [Anglin] used vile language and it was just raw hatred.'

However, there have been incidents in recent years where influencers have successfully held perpetrators to account. Broadcast journalist and BAFTA-award-winning documentary maker Mark Daly has received multiple threats on Twitter due to his work investigating issues within Scotland's Old Firm football clubs, Celtic and Rangers. In 2012, one attack that publicly revealed the address of his elderly parents prompted him to contact the police and the incident ended in the perpetrator being charged in court. 'Twitter is such a nefarious platform,' says Daly. 'If I didn't have a thick skin, I wouldn't be able to get out of bed in the morning thanks to the abuse I get from keyboard warriors behind anonymous avatars.'

The problem, says Wendling, is people have yet to learn how to behave online. 'We don't talk about standards of behaviour and social media companies have grown too fast to actually implement standards. The result is a culture of base emotions.'

Although banning trolls and discriminatory groups from social media may seem to be an effective way to deprive them of having influence, de-platforming simply relocates the offensive group – it doesn't solve the problem. Referring to an incel group that was banned from Reddit, Wendling says: 'Where do these guys congregate now? I don't know – but they're somewhere.'

THE CURIOUS CASE OF CLEMMIE HOOPER

Have you heard the story about the midwife who became a huge lifestyle influencer, was famously bullied off the internet and was then revealed to be a troll herself? This is the twisty tale of Clemmie Hooper, whose impressive Instagram career ended when she revealed she'd been sucked into the murky world of online forum bitching under an alias. Also known as Mother of Daughters, she'd fuelled scathing chats about her closest friends and even her husband, who were also influencers. These revelations occurred the year after she herself had experienced trolling so vicious, it left her on the 'verge of a breakdown'.

Hooper started building a digital audience in 2011 with her blog, Gas & Air, before joining Instagram in 2013. While the former was dedicated to sharing women's birth stories, her content took a distinctly more personal turn with the latter. She began posting home decor shots and pictures of her family: husband Simon, known online as Father of Daughters, and their children, Anya and Marnie. After discovering she was pregnant with twins, her audience snowballed and thousands of people followed her journey from mother of two to four when Ottilie and Delilah were born in 2016.

However, in September 2017, the internet turned against her via spiky threads on Mumsnet criticizing her for putting pictures of her children on Instagram. But then, so do thousands of people – why her? 'I don't know why I was targeted the most. I don't think I'm rude or aggressive,' she said. She joined the Mumsnet community, thinking her presence would defuse the situation and stop the 'horrible shouting' – but it didn't help. 'It got worse,' she said. 'I was so hurt – it took every bone in my body to not say how I was feeling. I felt broken, was being shouted at by a ring of women and couldn't make things any better.'

This experience had a significant impact on her mental health and in April 2018, Hooper disabled her Instagram account and digitally disappeared, pulling out of four significant brand deals in the process. A few months later – thanks to continuous messages of goodwill and a new sense of purpose – she returned. She relaunched her website, Gas & Air, and paid less attention to her personal Instagram. Through refocusing and building a small dedicated community around her blog, she seemed to have got her mojo back. 'I love having 40K followers instead of 600K,' she said. 'If

Instagram went away tomorrow, I wouldn't care as much – I will always be a midwife, I didn't set out to become an influencer.'

Then, one night in November 2019, Hooper confessed on Instagram Stories that she had become addicted to reading negative forums about her family on a website called Tattle Life and had joined the site to defend herself, under the pseudonym 'Alice In Wanderlust'. Except, as time went on, she became a troll herself, posting vicious comments about influencers with whom she'd been friends since early on in her digital career. In her confession – which was widely reported by mainstream media – she admitted she was full of regret.

Despite her husband also having a successful career as an influencer, his brand was severely damaged too. Gradually vanishing from the digital platforms they built, the Hoopers have gone from being Instagram stars to a cautionary tale. An example of how damaging the pursuit of digital popularity can be and how, behind the scenes, the influencer experience is far from the ideal it's portrayed to be.

Burnout: should the job come with a health warning?

Since 2016, a growing influencer problem has been burnout – when a content creator admits that, despite their life being everything they've ever dreamed of, they can't take it anymore. They are unhappy, suffering from mental health issues and buckling under the weight of a content creation schedule they have imposed upon themselves. Burnout is particularly prevalent among the most prolific YouTubers, who have built their subscriber bases and channels to a point where making videos can be their full-time job. The platform's most prolific creator, Felix Kjellberg – also known as PewDiePie – confessed he was suffering burnout in 2016, while four major influencers – Lilly Singh, Bobby Burns, Elle Mills and Rubén Gundersen – announced in 2018 they had to break off before they broke down. These announcements tend to be met with a mixture of compassion and impatience; however, the schedule many daily vloggers keep to maintain their upload pattern and volume of views involves few breaks and little sleep. For example, Tyler Blevins – better known as gaming streamer Ninja – revealed in an interview with YouTubers Ethan and Hila Klein for their podcast H3 that he is online everyday from 9.30 am until approximately 4:00 pm. Following this, he spends two or three hours with his family and then, from 7:00 pm until 2:00 am or 3:00 am, he is streaming game play. In 2018, he tweeted that forty-eight hours away from Twitch resulted in him losing 40,000 subscribers. As everyone interviewed for this book said: 'I wish you could see what goes in to this.'

Liam Chivers, founder of influencer agency OP Talent which represents prolific daily vloggers such as Ali-A, admits the routine a full-time YouTuber must adhere to is brutal and not necessarily good for the individual's health. He says: 'The general rule is you have to be uploading – if not every day, then a lot. Not just for engagement but to regularly get on to YouTube's homepage. Some guys worry and don't sleep if they think they might miss a day.'

Having witnessed the dedication and stamina required to maintain success on the platform, he has concluded some people are not suited to its demands, particularly in the world of gaming. 'They need to be winning every single day and the stress is real,' he says. 'If they don't get good game play in the first couple of hours, they might not get the views they need. It takes a certain type of character to handle that kind of pressure.'

Early-adopting YouTuber Taha Khan explains that to earn a living from the platform one must go after the mass 'roaming' audience who will deliver the views required to sustain a living from advertising revenue. These people discover content via the YouTube homepage and reviewing what is trending rather than necessarily subscribing to channels and investing time in being part of their communities.

Khan says: 'If you fall into the trap of following trends to get views, it never ends and that's where the burnout comes from. It's a spiral – you're chasing the roaming audience and you move away from why you started doing YouTube in the first place.'

Daily content creator Scott Major admits there is a relentlessness you must accept if you decide to make content creation your business. There are no breaks and several platforms to consider. 'Even when you're on holiday, you need to make sure you keep up to date with social media like Twitter and Instagram so your audience don't lose interest,' he says.

Chivers agrees that even a small amount of time away from YouTube for daily vloggers and producers can have a significant impact. 'Very few people get away with dropping off the radar,' he says. However, he does note there is an exception to the rule – one person, to whom in his experience algorithms and upload schedules make no difference: his client, KSI. 'People are constantly watching his back catalogue in the same way you might watch a box set,' he says.

Trust and audience proximity

While one of the most appealing aspects of influencers to their audiences is the friend-like nature of the relationship that is built between the two parties, this is also one of the most problematic. Unless the influencer treats their position with responsibility, their followers and subscribers can place a trust in them that is not only undeserved but leaves them in a vulnerable position. This is especially true and dangerous on YouTube, where prolific content creators with large audiences tend to be followed by a majority audience of children.

Speaking about the relationship between young subscribers and content creators, Khan says: 'I feel uncomfortable that young audiences don't see the performative nature of this. Because this is a performance.' As a result, he repeatedly includes an empty mug in his vlogs – cynically alluding to lifestyle

YouTubers frequently encouraging their followers to settle in with a cup of tea to watch their videos, as though they are friends about to have a juicy chat.

In 2018, an incident that received national press coverage in the UK was the accusations made by several teenage girls that Chris Ingham – father of daily vlogging YouTube channel The Ingham Family – had sent them suggestive and sexual messages on Twitter and Snapchat. One of his accusers, then sixteen-year-old Jess Simpson, claimed she received private messages from him while they were both staying at Disneyland Florida. She was with her parents, he was with his wife and children. In these messages, which she alleges are from Ingham, he encourages her to 'sneak out' to meet him and says he wants to go 'skinny dipping'. Uncomfortable with the tone of his communication, Simpson told her mother Theresa about the interactions and she later contacted Sussex Police, who said in a statement that, as Simpson was over sixteen years old, he had not committed an offence. Ingham denied all allegations in a video uploaded to YouTube in August 2018.

Since publicly sharing screenshots of the messages on Twitter, Simpson has revealed in her own YouTube video about the incident that she has received death threats from fans of The Ingham Family. Reading an open letter to Ingham, she says: 'You have no idea how damaging this is to me.'

The performative aspect of influencer content is often forgotten as they trade on their normality and relatability. They introduce their audience to their families and digitally invite them into their homes. Such openness does not elicit suspicion. However, even fellow influencers can be fooled when the idea that someone may be lying doesn't even cross their minds. This is what happened in the curious case of Asha Dawes, who was embraced by the parenting influencer community when she began sharing her story of being a mother with terminal cancer in 2017 using the name Asha Pinder. She became close friends and often collaborated with then-blogger Natasha Bailie. The only problem? It was a lie that not only facilitated her rise to digital prominence, but was part of a bigger scam in which she swindled £132,585.49 from her family for non-existent experimental health treatments and as part of an HMRC ruse she invented. In 2018, she was sentenced to four years in prison. Speaking about the incident in the aftermath, Bailie told Audrey Allan in an interview for her blog, Cancer With A Smile: 'I don't think anything can prepare you for finding out your friend has cancer, but absolutely nothing can prepare you for discovering that your friend who you were supporting and caring for lied to you about having cancer. It has been one of the most intense and sad years of my life.'

Identity creation, performance and yarn-spinning are the forte of the influencer as these skills allow them to turn everyday monotony into something worth tuning in for. Most slightly elevate their existing personalities to give their content energy, but there are others who portray themselves as individuals one can trust and then exploit their position. The fact is, the context of their delivery – a home just like yours, for example – implies safety and sincerity. They have nothing to hide. But as many influencers will admit, it's all construction.

The consequences of influencers giving the impression of something – as opposed to documenting the reality – were laid bare with the Fyre Festival fiasco of 2017. This was billed as a luxury music event due to take place across two weekends in April and May in the Bahamas and advertised via social content featuring and promoted by Kendall Jenner, Hailey Rhode Bieber and Bella Hadid. However, the reality of the festival – for which it cost up to $100,000 to attend – was rain-soaked mattresses, very little food and a setting which was essentially a building site. Documentaries of the disaster broadcast by Netflix and Hulu in 2019 portrayed Fyre Festival as a chaotic facade, organized by con artists and made to look desirable by influencers, who were basically acting as zero integrity guns for hire. Billy McFarland – the entrepreneur behind the event – was sentenced to six years in prison for fraud in 2018 and the more troubling lasting impact is his failure to pay the local people who worked on Fyre Festival, some of whom even stumped up costs using their life savings.

And as for the influencers? Jillionaire, a DJ and producer, succinctly described the promotion and appeal of the event in an interview for Netflix's documentary as being like 'Instagram coming to life' and, according to the BBC, Kendall Jenner alone was reportedly paid $250,000 to publish one post on her feed which – in the controversial aftermath of the event – she deleted. While many people working in influencer marketing have spun Fyre Festival as proof of how effective influencers actually are at driving sales, others have used it to springboard conversations about content creators signposting paid promotion in a coherent and consistent way. Jenner's Instagram post about Fyre Festival? It was not labelled as sponsored. For others, it has confirmed everything they already believed about influencers – that they exist to drive a kind of consumerism that suggests being like them is important. Meme-maker Mollie Goodfellow says: 'It's everything about influencer culture that I hate. It was basically the effect of people saying we're better than you but you could get like this if you part with your money.'

Influencer scandals followed by quick apologies have become commonplace on social media due to a high frequency of inappropriate historic tweets being uncovered and content creators being seemingly unaware when their actions are culturally unacceptable. Although this has led to a noisy 'cancellation culture' – when the online mob unanimously decides an influencer is no longer worthy of their attention – in most cases it has not dented their audience size or impacted on the flow of money towards them. Despite using racist language on multiple occasions, beauty YouTuber Jeffree Star continues to garner high-profile brand deals, such as his 2019 collaboration with make-up brand Morphe Cosmetics. The uncovering of racist and classist historic tweets published by Zoe Sugg, Jack Maynard and Holly Boon have not halted sponsorship and collaboration opportunities for them. Meanwhile, KSI has trivialized rape and used misogynistic language, while Alfie Deyes' vlog about living on a pound for a day featured his personal trainer and him complaining about drinking tap water. Every influencer scandal generates a huge amount of noise on Twitter and, in the cases of the most prominent content creators, even results in mainstream media coverage. However, does it slow commercial interest in what they are offering? No. The uncomfortable truth is, if an influencer's direct audience does not seem to care and supports them no matter what, the flow of money towards them facilitating their content will continue.

But what if the numbers aren't what they seem to be?

The issue that dominated the influencer marketing industry in 2018 was influencer fraud – the practice of influencers buying bot-filled audiences and engagement and then generating revenue from this through brand deals. At Cannes Lion the same year, then Unilever chief marketing officer Keith Weed appealed for urgent action and transparency and vowed the company would no longer work with influencers who bought followers. He said the practice of buying audiences from bot farms was eroding trust between consumers and influencers, which is the very reason brands find these individuals valuable. Meanwhile, in the same year Kellogg's announced it intended to stop basing influencer fees on their reach as it could not be certain apparent engagement was real. The company has instead moved towards valuing content creators based on their aesthetic, tone of voice and how their audience demographics relate to its target market. There has been a sense brands must be seen to be taking action to save face having potentially had the wool pulled over their eyes by dishonest agencies and individuals. A 2019 study by Captiv8 – a San Francisco influencer technology startup – revealed $2.1bn was spent on sponsored influencer Instagram posts in 2017 but 11 per cent of the engagement this activity generated came from fake accounts.

But it's not just brands who have taken action to tackle influencer fraud – it's social platforms too. As a result of Twitter identifying and clearing out fake followers in 2018, Lady Gaga's audience decreased by 2.5 million people. Facebook deactivated 2.2 billion accounts the following year for the same reason and Instagram began deleting users it believed to be bots.

However, although Weed grabbed headlines for his hardcore, no fake followers stance in 2018, influencers themselves had been calling out the practice of buying audiences and engagement since the beginning of 2017. They could see waves of people springing up after the 2015 Instagram influencer boom when it became clear having a significant following on the platform was a viable route to a lucrative career and luxury lifestyle. And, for those who had been blogging and vlogging since the early days – and were intimately acquainted with the length of time it takes to build an engaged audience – they adopted an 'us and them' position. In the same way almost every content creator interviewed believes the term 'influencer' is too broad because it does not recognize the very individual careers they have carved for themselves, they also find the exploitation of the digital landscape they created dangerous as, thanks to their catch-all job title, it means the entire community stands to suffer thanks to this behaviour. The overwhelming message that has emerged from fraudulent audience building is that one cannot trust influencers as a whole. Publicly policing and calling this out when it first became widespread was their way of warning their commercial partners and setting themselves apart from those who were scamming the system.

One influencer, who asked not to be named, revealed buying followers is now much less common than buying Instagram engagement as even established content creators struggle to get visibility in the platform's feed due to algorithm changes which prioritize volume of likes and comments.

Victoria McGrath, founder of Inthefrow, shared a blog on her website explaining why influencers with fake followings were bad news for both consumers and brands and gave advice on how to spot when influencers had bought their audiences. Despite being significantly different from her usual combination of fashion, travel and beauty content, she felt she had to take a stand. In the post, she said: 'It comes down to this; many of us have spent years (6 years for me) building a genuine audience on our social channels. People who found us and followed us for our content and creativity.'

Entrepreneur, interior stylist and blogger Sarah Akwisombe was early to call out influencer fraud in 2017 and did so, first, because 'people shouldn't treat the public like idiots' and, second, it 'creates a cynicism and negativity within what should and could be quite a fun world'. She adds: 'It creates a false economy – a "bubble" inside the Instagram economy that means people think "I need to do that too as that's how it works". Also, not everyone is as clued up enough to realize what's going on.'

Meanwhile, for brands trying to navigate the space and discern between authentic and bought audiences, methods and tools for spotting influencer fraud have been wilfully simplistic at best and inaccurate at worst. A common piece of advice is to look for audience number surges; however, one must take into consideration the context in which that influencer's following may have grown. Have they launched a new product or collaborated with a more prolific content creator? For example, when Annabel Rivkin and Emilie McMeekan – founders of The Midult – released their first book in September 2018, their following soared by approximately 6,000 people over the course of three days. This was due to organic promotion by fellow influencers whose content was aimed at the same demographic as theirs and coverage by mainstream media. While some influencer tech tools would deem this to be a red flag, in reality The Midult at that very moment was presenting an exciting brand opportunity. Meanwhile, influencer engagement can spike due to the nature of the content they have published – for example, weddings, engagements and newborns outperform every other kind of post. The conclusion? Investigate who you are working with. Review their platforms manually, with your own eyes. You will be amazed at what a quick Google search surfaces – and it could be the difference between career-making campaign and a corporate disaster.

HOW TO SPOT A BOUGHT AUDIENCE: THREE TOP TIPS

1 Dozens of comments that are simply emojis or one-word responses. Comments that have poor grammar or are in a different language to the influencer's native tongue are also a tell-tale sign. Ideally, you want to work with influencers whose audiences ask questions, tag friends and share personal information. In this situation, an influencer who is responding to comments and driving the conversation is also a positive sign.

2 A large audience with extremely poor engagement. This suggests the followers have been bought en masse from a bot farm and as they then do not engage with the content, it is getting zero visibility in the newsfeeds of Instagram or Facebook or the explore page of Instagram.

3 Enormous audience growth in a short space of time (for example, zero to 100,000). Anyone who has built a social audience from scratch knows that getting to the first 10,000 followers on any platform is gruelling – organically, it can take up to a year. Look back at influencers' content and discover the moment they started to gain traction. Is their growth plausible? Did they collaborate with a better-known influencer or did something they posted go viral? Also, consider who they are connected to – a large and instantly engaged audience is possible if the person in question is dating, related to or working with someone prolific.

FIVE INFLUENCER CONTROVERSIES THAT MADE MAINSTREAM NEWS

Miroslava Duma: in 2018, entrepreneur and founder of fashion website Buro 24/7 received a backlash after posting a card she received from designer Ulyana Sergeenko on Instagram Stories that featured racist language. A few days later, a video from 2012 was uncovered and went viral in which Duma expressed concern about men wearing women's clothing and her belief certain imagery should be censored. Her most high-profile critics included Naomi Campbell and blogger Bryanboy, who she declared in the video to be 'weird'.

Claudia Oshry Soffer: the founder of meme-focused Instagram and podcast Girl With No Job, Soffer was the subject of negative press when it broke that her mother – Pamela Geller – was an anti-Muslim activist. Although she announced she did not hold the same views as Geller, several anti-Muslim posts from her social platforms were soon uncovered and her talk show *The Morning Breath* was cancelled.

Jeffree Star: leaked messages and videos in 2017 and 2018 showed the beauty YouTuber repeatedly using racist language and, in one incident, appears to refer to fellow vlogger Jackie Aina as a 'gorilla'. In response, Aina penned an open letter to Star on Twitter in which she called his actions 'blatantly racist' and his comments made mainstream news.

Shane Dawson: the YouTuber has weathered many controversies since starting his digital content career back in the days of Myspace. However, he was forced to apologize in 2019 after comments about bestiality which he made in 2015 on his podcast Shane and Friends re-emerged. This follows his apology in 2018 for paedophilia jokes he also made on his podcast from an episode in 2013.

Yovana Mendoza: despite promoting the benefits of a raw, vegan diet on YouTube and Instagram, Mendoza was caught on camera eating fish in 2019. In a vlog filmed to explain the incident – for which she received a significant backlash – she revealed her decision to start eating animal products was the result of health issues. However, critics had little sympathy for her, as instead of independently admitting to changing her lifestyle she continued advising her audience to follow the raw vegan diet she suspected may be making her unwell.

KEY TAKEAWAYS

- An influencer's community can quickly turn into an online mob if they disagree with something the influencer has said or done. Bear in mind that this is the age of being offended, in which one accusation of insensitivity or ignorance can snowball within hours.
- For YouTubers who approach their channels as a full-time job, uploading videos regularly – ideally on a daily basis – is necessary to maintain the

views required to make an income from the platform. They have to quickly jump on trending topics and content formats if they are to get visibility on the YouTube homepage, which is crucial to picking up engagement from the platform's mass, roaming audience. Even an enormously engaged following can drop off if a content creator fails to post for up to one week.

- YouTuber burnout is a growing issue among daily vloggers as they struggle to produce and edit new content every day for various social platforms. A creator's upload schedule is worth bearing in mind as, if you as a brand are investing in a partnership with a YouTuber, ideally you need them to maintain that schedule to ensure the content you have invested in continues to get visibility.

- Find out who you are working with. Do they have past controversies? Have they been the subject of scandal? Also, do they make the same mistakes repeatedly? Brand association with influencers who have shared discriminatory views is not only bad for image, but bad for business too as it stands to isolate your company from entire communities.

- Investigate audience engagement and growth with your own eyes and use common sense. If the amount of likes and comments seems implausible in relation to the audience size, there is a chance they are; but equally there may be a reason for a sudden surge in popularity that could signal this influencer at this point in time is presenting an exciting brand opportunity.

9

The future of digital influence

Fact: digital influence is here to stay. The industry that has sprung up around it will change and how people operate as influencers will evolve, but as long as consumers use the internet, there will be digital influencers. As long as brands need to communicate with consumers, there will be a flow of money towards the influencer industry that allows it to grow. The two things that are set to fundamentally change are what individuals use their influence for and how they use the platforms at their disposal to do this.

Talk to any influencer with significant success and they will tell you they are moving towards a frame of mind that is more platform agnostic: it doesn't really matter where the content is published, the point is they will always publish content. 'It's not necessarily about YouTube or Instagram – they could come and go – but the concept of sharing communication online is here to stay,' says YouTuber, author and entrepreneur Patricia Bright. 'This will probably always be part of my life in some way.' Meanwhile, Devran Karaca – founder of Kyra TV which produces influencer-led content – admits his ambition is not just to simply grow his brand on major social channels but is eyeing bigger opportunities. 'We're looking at streaming services and licensing,' he says. It's not quite traditional media but it's also a step beyond the algorithmic chaos and democracy of YouTube. In fact, association with a specific platform is something many influencers – particularly early adopters – are keen to shake off and interest in crossing over to traditional media remains high on their list of goals. YouTuber and author Louise Pentland would ultimately like to be a contestant on BBC One reality competition *Strictly Come Dancing* or a panellist on ITV chat show *Loose Women* while blogger and stylist LaTonya Staubs, whose first book was published in 2019, is keen to explore where she as a writer could go. Although she says she will continue to use social media, she is 'focused on writing and building that portion of myself'. Similarly, author and blogger Katherine Ormerod would ideally like to work on a second book and a screenplay but expects she and many people like her will continue to have layered, multi-hyphenate careers. 'I will always write because it is a pure joy. I'll work with brands and do consultancy as well as taking work as a speaker,' she says. 'I want to mix all of these things.'

Calgary Avansino – *Vogue* editor turned influencer turned startup CEO – believes the idea of traditional media is changing as the current wave of social platforms (YouTube, Facebook, Twitter and Instagram) begin to reach maturity. 'Maybe someday soon we'll be referring to Facebook as traditional,' she muses. However, as the founder of Glamcam – a beauty game show app focused on make-up – who is now operating in the world of technology, she does see a change in user desires that may impact on the kind of social platforms the next wave of influencers emerge on. She notes consumers are looking for 'less horizontal, broad platforms and more focused communities' which are specific to their interests. She adds: 'The world of tech in its essence is about change, innovation and improvement, so it is challenging to deem anyone king eternally.' However, in her view, Instagram's ability to continually delight people – despite its issues – means it's going nowhere. Karaca agrees, but advises brands who are trying to reach the demographic classed as Generation Z or younger to remember that watching YouTube is 'ingrained' into their behaviour. For some, it feels more natural than turning on the television.

However, it is worth noting this book focuses almost squarely on influencers and behaviour in the West and there are wealthy markets elsewhere in which the potential of this industry has yet to be fully exploited. For example, there are currently fewer fashion and beauty influencers coming out of the United Arab Emirates and Saudi Arabia – despite consumer desire for luxury lifestyle content – as discretion is valued so highly in the region. Louise Nichol, who was editor-in-chief of *Harper's Bazaar Arabia* from 2009 until 2018, suspects it will not stay this way forever. 'I expect, as society evolves, this will likely change,' she says. To be a successful luxury lifestyle influencer here, Nichol adds it is imperative to appeal to the wealthy Khaleeji consumer – those living in the Arabian Peninsula – which means demonstrating a combination of impeccable taste and strong family values. 'Karen Wazen Bakhazi is a good example of this,' she says. 'Lebanese influencers tend to dominate the luxury field.'

Her tip for brands and potential influencers eyeing the region? 'There will likely be a shift towards more Arabic-language content as the Kingdom of Saudi Arabia opens up. If someone can crack an aspirational, yet relevant, Arabic proposition they will likely do very well.'

Legacy, truth and treasuring small audiences

For influencers who were either early adopters or gathered audience during the 2014–15 Instagram boom, the idea of quality and permanence weighs heavily. They have built their careers around volume, the ability to be nimble and a talent for moment-to-moment publishing. However, for many, this churn is no longer satisfying and they are seeking projects that offer time and space to produce long-lasting work with meaning. Despite benefiting from being an early adopter of Instagram, photographer Jonathan Daniel Pryce, known as Garcon Jon, is reacquainting himself with the analogue techniques that sparked his love of photography when he was a student and learned how to develop imagery in a dark room. 'I'm using film photography more and more and investing in a slower process,' he says. 'Posting hundreds of pictures interests me much less, and actually I'd like to do more books.'

Fellow photographer and early Instagram user Finn Beales is also finding there is significant interest in his work following a personal project for which he printed a book of photography about his life in Hay-on-Wye, Wales. After years of chasing likes, views and algorithms, there is a sense that compromising integrity and creative vision to please the masses is no longer the god influencers are so keen to serve. Early to this realization was Jack Harries, co-founder of YouTube channel JacksGap turned environmental activist and film-maker, who described in a 2017 talk for The Do Lectures the mental dissatisfaction of simply being driven by volume. He describes the pressure to publish more content on YouTube as 'incessant' and reflecting on the panic he felt as his channel grew, he says he remembers thinking: 'how do you keep this many people happy?' A renewed appreciation for small communities and more targeted projects away from the catch-all genre of lifestyle was made clear again and again during influencer interviews.

Meanwhile, after years of composition and perfection-focused images on Instagram, there is a move towards a more realistic, less deliberate aesthetic. This is due to content creators attempting to get cut-through as the platform becomes more congested and a devil-may-care approach to imagery and video from Generation Z. Indeed, content formats favoured by millennials that have been synonymous with Instagram – flatlays, suspiciously flawless bodies and blemish-free selfies – are being challenged by an emerging style which is blurry, nonchalant and altogether more grunge. Pryce says: 'Younger people are not taking it as seriously as we have. I look at Billie Eilish, who is this anti-social media star and part of a generation who looks at the platform the way we look at Facebook: it's for your parents. It's not cool to try as hard as we have.'

On the flipside, those influencers who gathered audiences through publishing aspirational content are also moving towards a grittier documentation of their lives. Not just for engagement, but because they want to develop a deeper connection with their followers and are troubled by the impact Insta-perfection has had on real life.

Jennifer Dickinson, digital editorial director of NET-A-PORTER, says she is seeing a drift towards vulnerability in the social content that many influencers are posting. This is also a key theme in the work of New Zealand artist Ruby Jones, whose heartfelt illustration marking the 2019 Christchurch mosque terrorist attack encapsulated the global feeling of grief to such an extent it went viral, having been shared by celebrities such Gigi Hadid. Speaking of her illustrations, she said: 'They are meant to show tiny glimpses into real human moments, I think people need that and I think that is why they connect with my pictures.'

Violet Gaynor, co-founder of parenting website The Glow, says the brand has gone through a natural evolution which has been informed by her own experience of motherhood. She believes her followers are looking for content that elicits an emotional response and makes them feel supported. 'People are seeking truth and the more raw it is the better because that's what we go through,' she says. 'It's saying "you're not the only one in the bathroom crying and hiding it from your children". Saying you're not the only person going through this is a powerful thing to say.'

Also tapping into an aesthetic that is more rooted in reality than an Instagram-friendly aesthetic is celebrity stylist turned fashion industry critic Grace Woodward, who has seen a surge in her Instagram engagement since beginning her project Body of Work – a series of nudes depicting her own unfiltered body. She launched this to counter the huge volume of nudity already on the platform, which she likens to porn, out of fear for how this is shaping perception of the female form.

'People are crying out for honesty and are less able to deal with real life because they are not seeing it represented,' she says. 'You can't be what you can't see and all you see on Instagram is sexualized women. You see so many women on there looking for validation.'

For some influencers, developing a rawer aesthetic and narrative online isn't enough for them to feel like they are providing the service their community needs. To extend the conversations they have started, they are taking their brands in a new direction: offline. Clemmie Telford, parenting influencer and founder of website Mother of All Lists, says: 'I'm making what I do live – taking it into the real world where people can tell stories in a room, share experiences and hug each other.'

Human interaction and facilitating face-to-face discussion is a major focus for influencers who have seen their audiences open up as a result of sharing content that rebels against the clichéd gloss of Instagram. Founders of The Midult, Annabel Rivkin and Emilie McMeekan, discovered through a series of events organized to promote their first book, *I'm Absolutely Fine! A Manual for Imperfect Women*, that their followers were in actual fact not fine and desperately wanted to talk about it. Attendees were encouraged to complete the sentence 'I'm absolutely fine, but...' written on cards that were distributed at the start of each meet-up and the confessional outpouring was extraordinary. Responses included, 'I feel overlooked and undervalued', 'I'm the most isolated person I know' and 'my boss is a corporate psychopath and I feel too old to look for another one'.

Ahead of the curve in her dedication to documenting what is real was Poorna Bell. Following writing about her husband's suicide for HuffPost in 2015 and receiving an outpouring of online gratitude for the space this opened up for discussion about mental health, she has vowed not to share content that follows trends or is clichéd. 'I don't post anything that feels like a lie, it literally makes my skin crawl,' she says. 'I'm not going to say I feel empowered when I don't.'

However, none of this means the fashion-focused, perfectly styled content popularized by millennial influencers will disappear. Instagram editorial is set to evolve and represent people who are seeking more than lifestyle inspiration but its status as an ever-growing lookbook is here to stay and this is without doubt a positive thing for brands. As Dickinson points out: 'There are influencers who people really shop from, they are so knowledgeable and truly understand which brands work for them.' So defined is Instagram as a platform for fashion and lifestyle, early adopter Ramona Jones says 'more than ever' she sees it as a shopping platform, despite this being at odds with the travel and slow-living focus of her own content.

For brands in this market to grow, however, they do have to consider messaging and the influencers they are working with to entice new consumers to their products. Plus-size fashion blogger Chloe Elliott notes that bandwagoning on topical areas of discussion such as diversity without demonstrating full representation in campaigns will no longer be acceptable. A former buyer for the fashion industry, she is also suspicious that many brands producing work focused on this narrative do not understand what body positivity is and their campaigns are actually damaging as they reveal corporate ignorance. 'Only brands that truly want to be inclusive and show diversity will succeed in using the body positivity message,' she says. 'I want to see more plus-size women, disabled people, trans people – we don't all come in "one size" and it's time that brands started showing that and fully representing their customer base.' It makes sense to explore this market from a financial, not just an image perspective too, given the plus-size womenswear market in the US alone is worth $46bn. From her position as both an influencer and working in-house as a social content producer for British fashion brand Boden, Lucy Nicholls can testify the desire for and power of inclusion is real. 'People are definitely demanding that brands be more representative and more people with a point of view are rising up,' she says.

Generation Z and using digital influence to change the world

The millennial and xennial influencer anxiety that – despite high engagement and large audiences – they are preaching to the converted, particularly on Twitter, has been exploded by Generation Z's approach to social media and using digital platforms to show, tell and mobilize. The strategies of content creators and commentators from this demographic suggest a more innate understanding of how to use social media and motivate their audiences than previous generations have demonstrated. In addition, rather than being divided by partisan politics, they are united by issues that stand to impact on their generation, and even cut their lives short; most prominently, climate change, violence, racism and mental health. While the millennial influencer reaction to the global chaos they came of age in – an economy ravaged by the global recession – was to create a career via social media that took them away from the hopelessness of it, Generation Z influencers are determined to engage with macro issues and be part of the solution.

Take Emma González, a survivor of the 2018 shootings at Marjory Stoneman Douglas High School in Parkland, Florida, who became a figurehead of the March for Our Lives movement in America, established the year of the attack to push for gun control and legislative reform. Rather than campaign on the platforms most used by her generation – YouTube, Instagram and Snapchat – she headed to Twitter. This was a fight that required oxygen from mainstream media and politicians. And where are they? Twitter. She wrote a first-person piece for *The New York Times* about being an activist, thus owning the narrative about her experience both online and offline in places where her target readers – the legislators and media companies – were likely to be looking. The column – entitled 'Vote, shave your head and cry whenever you need to' – was a harrowing read which, due to being entirely from her perspective instead of being given context by a journalist, made it immediately possible to understand the trauma she and her classmates had experienced. 'Even when people come up to us quietly to say thank you, you never know if they're just trying to shoot you at close range,' she wrote. The piece went viral on Facebook and Twitter, and she and her fellow survivors toured America in 2018 encouraging young people who wanted to end gun violence to vote. In addition, the March for Our Lives demonstration in March of the same year, which took place in a series of events across the US, was the largest youth protest since that against the Vietnam War. Politicians keen to capture the youth vote in the 2020 election – when González and her peers will be present at the ballot boxes for the first time – are now in no doubt about the issue this demographic feels strongly about.

Similarly, Swedish environmental activist Greta Thunberg has millions of followers across Facebook, Twitter and Instagram. This allows her to demonstrate that her agenda to push for political action against climate change is one supported by an audience too large to ignore. However, she has also spoken at the UN and the World Economic Forum in Davos – not to appeal to world leaders and politicians but to warn them her generation will continue to take action until they do. 'Since our leaders are behaving like children, we will have to take the responsibility they should have taken long ago,' she said at the UN Summit in 2018. Her activism career began in August that year when instead of going to school she sat outside the Swedish parliament to protest against the lack of political action being taken against climate change. Since then, 20,000 children have initiated school strikes around the world and there was a global climate school strike in which 1.2 million children participated on 15 March 2019. Politicians such as the UK's Theresa May and Australia's Scott Morrison have criticized striking children and encouraged them to get back to school. While this is not the reaction activists might want, the fact these strikes have been acknowledged in the quarters of decision makers is without doubt having a ripple effect, an influence. At her TED Talk in December 2018, Thunberg highlighted: 'If a few children can get headlines just by not going to school for a few weeks, imagine what we could all do together if you wanted to.' She has not only proved someone her age can have influence but created a template for others of her age to replicate. Doing and saying, showing and telling, social media and traditional media. This generation are approaching influence – and the things they could have influence over – in a much more rigorous way than their predecessors.

For Finn Harries – who first became prominent online in 2012 as co-founder of YouTube channel JacksGap – engaging with the climate fight began due to a personal experience at the beginning of his design degree in 2015. He has since campaigned as part of activist group Extinction Rebellion, made a documentary with the WWF about the effects of climate change on the Greenland ice sheet and given talks at the UN.

He says: 'I walked into my first architecture class where I was asked to design a flood barrier for rising sea levels. Despite having grown up learning about the effects of a warmer climate, this was the first time that I realized how fundamentally this problem will shape my life.'

This project – as well as reading work by environmentalists such as Bill McKibben and theorist Jeremy Rifkin – 'propelled' him to take action. He notes in the four-year period that has followed his first assignment, carbon emissions have continued to rise, global temperature continues to break records and there have been no effective policy changes. 'This movement has become the single biggest challenge my generation will face in their lifetime,' he says.

Interestingly, he believes his peers – like millennials before them – are still using social platforms to promote an aspirational lifestyle, it's just that this lifestyle is climate mobilization. 'Young people are looking for a sense of purpose and meaning in their life – that's what activism can offer,' he says. 'At a time where loneliness, depression and anxiety are at an all-time high, there is a real hunger for community and shared values. Documenting the climate mobilization publicly on social media helps build a sense of community and common purpose between people who may be thousands of miles apart.'

While Harries highlights Thunberg's work as 'an incredible example of the power that one individual holds when their actions are amplified through social media channels', Alice Aedy, an activist, documentary maker and photojournalist, deems her 'remarkable'. Aedy has also protested against the lack of political action against climate change and shares this and her photography on Instagram.

She says: 'I hope this translates into genuine systemic change. I can only think of the years of activism that have occurred in environmental circles to little avail, and some spectacular viral moments such as the image of Alan Kurdi which failed to truly solicit the political response to the refugee crisis that was required.'

Although she finds the effect of social media on environmental activism encouraging, she is concerned by the context in which people are accessing information about devastating global issues on these platforms. 'What is the impact of seeing an image from a bombing in Syria in between a cat meme and photo of Beyoncé?' she says. 'Does the way we consume that content trivialize the issue at hand?' She believes being 'more humanizing than ever' when it comes to reporting is critical to ensure people cannot be reduced to numbers.

That is not to say Generation Z in its entirety is mobilized towards using social media and their influence to catalyse global change. While the demographic seems to unite under banner issues, YouTuber Taha Khan argues that he and many of his peers have become less politically active since 2018 due to a 'shocking and outraging' political awakening, which happened in 2016 following Britain's decision to leave the European Union and the presidential election in America of Donald Trump. He says: 'We're burned out by the fatigue of trying to keep up with politics. Especially when it comes to Trump – something new happens every day. It has been like an information fire hose, many of us just can't do it anymore.'

As a result of this data burnout, he has muted political words on Twitter so that he can use the platform while avoiding triggering conversations. And

Khan is not the only one taking measures to protect his mental health in the face of second-to-second news – according to global market research agency Mintel, 21 per cent of consumers in the UK alone have cut the time they are spending on social media for the same reason.

Despite seemingly polarized levels of political engagement, he highlights that his generation is united by the fact it is an 'ideas-focused' one whose online currency is 'memes, jokes and having interesting things to say'. 'These have high value,' he says. Also, while the internet and Twitter feels fast, Facebook and Instagram – to him – feel slow and not current enough to be places where his generation will congregate online in the future. However, he does make one thing clear: they are constantly consuming content – be it visually or audibly – and it feels unnatural to simply be doing nothing. 'We have always had the option to not be bored,' he says. 'I have no memory of ever being bored.'

This suggests brands may have to start experimenting across different platforms and thinking about the kind of content they are producing in collaboration with influencers – and for their own platforms – if they are to tap into Gen Z. Since 2015 at least, there has been such a focus on achieving success on Instagram but shorter form-focused platforms such as TikTok – which allow users to create fifteen-second videos – have gained traction because they are Vine-like and fun. The app was downloaded 68 million times in October 2018 alone, which was a year-on-year increase of 395 per cent.

Considering the 'burnout' Khan detailed from consuming constant political and topical information from Twitter, it makes sense that a platform more focused on momentary entertainment has appealed to his generation. However, similar to Vine, nothing on TikTok is high production and harks back to this aforementioned idea that social media is moving into an era of anti-perfection. In an interview with *Variety* in November 2018, the company's head of global marketing, Stefan Heinrich Henriquez, said what he loved about the platform was that consumers were using it to 'show their real side'.

Regardless of which platform Generation Z influencers use, the main reason they are going to change what social content looks like and what social media is for is because they are not following the path set by millennials. Up until this point, brands and users have taken this as gospel – this is what an Instagram post should look like, these are the content formats one must use for YouTube. Flatlays, selfies, shopping hauls, get ready with me videos – they have dominated the landscapes of Instagram and YouTube. However, with Generation Z using social platforms in a different way – looking outward instead of turning the camera on themselves and utilizing online platforms to create offline mass mobilization – it is inevitable social content is going to change too. In her TED Talk about climate change, Thunberg summed up their perspective succinctly: 'The rules have to change, everything has to change, and it has to start today.'

Innovating to achieve digital influence

Micro vs macro. Engagement vs reach. Likes, comments and shares. We have become obsessed with terminology in the influencer industry without considering what this means and how useful it is to us. To begin, the definitions of micro and macro influencers must be standardized if they are to be universally understood and helpful. While one business may define micro as an individual with 25,000 followers, another might position it as someone with an audience of 100,000. There are vastly different views on what it means to be small.

Meanwhile, there is also the question of whether or not the audience size actually matters, as for many brands – particularly those in luxury or niche markets – the challenge is reaching the correct demographics, not the largest. By present standards, one might pay a five-figure sum for a sponsored video from a YouTuber with millions of subscribers. However, given how young the majority audience is on the platform, it could be argued that reaching all of those eyeballs has little value unless the brand is affordable for, aimed at and suitable to the younger consumer. If not, what is the value in working with a mass influencer? Why pay a large amount of money for a large number of people if they are not your target audience? Also, as mentioned in Chapter 7, the idea of mass itself is in decline as consumers take a more individualistic approach to identity, lifestyle and where they spend their time online. If one is not trying to reach a mass youth audience, and a breakdown of said influencer's audience demographics reveals that just 10 per cent of the people who engaged with the content were of the target demographic, has the campaign been worth the spend for the brand? In fact, partnering with someone who has a smaller, more targeted audience may be more efficient and worth more despite the difference in numbers. Regardless of audience size and reach, communicating with the correct audience via an influencer who has parallel views and an aesthetic consistent with the brand's is more valuable than a mass following who is there to be entertained. It goes back to the concepts of digital celebrity and authoritative influence explained in Chapter 1 which are based on an individual's motivation for following an influencer rather than assuming numerical popularity means influence. Thinking in terms of entertainment vs authority and mass vs niche will allow us to get closer to creating the kind of partnerships that strongly reinforce brand and deliver value. Continuing to spend big money on big numbers without truly understanding what those numbers mean in the context of individual campaigns means the aim of the industry will continually be tied to mass, and in an era of growing individualism it may be wiser to consider something much more niche.

And what about the word 'influencer' . . .?

Every interview for this book has surfaced an opinion on the term 'influencer'. Rather than people being uncomfortable with the idea that they have digital influence, they are more concerned with how one job title for thousands of people providing different functions flattens this industry. They also hate the hierarchy it suggests and some feel it indicates a level of self-importance they do not necessarily feel. Pentland believes there is a stigma attached to the word that will only disappear with time and education and Olivia Purvis – founder of blog and YouTube channel What Olivia Did – is 'conflicted' on using it to describe herself. She also thinks it is something of a blow to early adopters like herself who have been building their audiences and legacies for a significant period of time. 'I understand why it's such an easy word to use,' she says. 'Equally, I think it negates a lot of the hard work and skill set so many people have poured into this profession before Instagram or "influencing" was a thing.'

Meanwhile, Dickinson has abandoned using the term as she does not think it fairly represents the impact they are having across various industries. 'The good ones are their own brands. Also, what they do is hard work – it takes so much time and is of real value,' she says. However, she does believe it would be wise for those working in fashion on Instagram and blogs to consider adding YouTube to their repertoire as the style content there, in her opinion, could be better. 'There is a lot of room for improvement,' she says. 'Some of the beauty channels are brilliant, but I wouldn't go there for style. That is obviously an opportunity.'

Interestingly, influencers are now polarized on how to take their careers forward – on one hand there are many who see it as a long-term proposition and have no plans to diversify or put a deadline on their tenure in the field, despite pleas from their friends and families, concerned about the stability of an industry so new.

Those who've ridden waves of algorithm changes, content trends and platform upgrades and have spent a significant amount of time growing audiences on their existing platforms. Ramona Jones – who focuses most on her blog and Instagram – says she would be happy with 'more of the same'.

'People say I shouldn't put all of my eggs into one basket but you would do that with any other career. I'm happy to put all my eggs in one basket,' she says.

Meanwhile, even though Kat Farmer – also known as Does My Bum Look 40 in This? – has made broadcasting via Instagram Stories a cornerstone of her offering alongside blogging and permanent Instagram grid content, YouTube holds no appeal for her despite the commercial opportunities the platform could certainly offer. Known for cornering the market of fashion content for women in their forties, her resolve to stick with what she knows comes from instinct about what her audience wants. 'I think we're very much still TV people,' she says. 'I'm not convinced how engaged my audience is with YouTube.'

And on the other hand? There are influencers who believe the sky is the limit and creating content is simply part of a much bigger ambition. Fashion blogger and entrepreneur Elle Ferguson has no plans to slow her social media but her mission is much more related to her beauty product line Elle Effect. 'My ultimate goal is to have at least one product in every woman's bathroom cupboard,' she says.

Similarly, 'empire-building' is Patricia Bright's square focus and this isn't necessarily related to YouTube – after all, she already did this successfully with her extensions company Y-Hair, which operated as a completely separate business from her personal brand. As far as the future goes? 'I'm interested in education, self-improvement and helping women understand what their opportunities are,' she says.

Katherine Ormerod believes the non-linear career of influencers is symptomatic of what people want from workplaces now, and a 2019 survey in which found 17 per cent of eleven- to sixteen-year-olds interviewed in a group of 2,000 want to be influencers when they leave school. Their reasons for this choice were fame, money and enjoyment. As first-generation influencer manager Liam Chivers observes, lifestyle attainability is part of the reason his client base is so successful. 'People feel like theirs are stories they can aspire to and there's no reason why they can't become a YouTuber,' he says.

For Ormerod, the freedom and flexibility of a plural career has been too fulfilling for her to return to a more rigid, 9:00 am to 5:00 pm situation. She says: 'I truly believe I'm unemployable now. The way I want to live and work is incompatible with a traditional office environment. A lot of people have my attitude and I truly believe it's going to be a problem for businesses in the future.'

She also thinks her move to build a career which is specific to her rather than take a full-time position at a brand is down to the fact 'the workplace doesn't work for women', particularly post-motherhood. 'At least nobody can sack me while I'm on maternity leave,' she says. 'At the end of the day, it comes down to this: are you going to get out there and earn your own money on your own terms or wait for someone to pay you? I actually think it's a feminist issue.'

For Eman Kellam – an early-adopting Generation Z YouTuber – having a plural career feels like a natural thing to do, essentially because this is the norm for his peers. 'I guess my generation were lucky enough to be born in the age of the internet,' he says. 'There are jobs that don't even exist yet which will become available and we are the generation creating these jobs. We will most definitely have several of them at the same time.' Kellam cites KSI as a good example of how his generation of influencers will ideally approach their careers moving forward. 'He's written a book, has a clothing line, he's an actor and he raps, among other things.'

This desire to continue down the rabbit hole of digital publishing, build an audience and pursue the adjacent opportunities it seems to inevitably bring appears to be the most trodden path for individuals successfully utilizing their digital influence. The one exception interviewed was Lucy Nicholls who – although she was an early adopter of blogging and social media, not to mention part of a fashion ecosystem of equally successful influencers – walked away from this as a potential career. 'I don't regret it,' she says. 'But I am so thankful I did it. It has given me the best opportunities that I never would have had if I hadn't started blogging. I got all my jobs in my career from being an influencer.'

This is an interesting point and something that has become more important in many jobs related to publishing since approximately 2014 – a significant personal social following. Not only does this prove, in theory, the ability to grow an online audience but it gives brands that need it another avenue to promote content. In addition, for traditional publishers, having in-house influencers when putting together brand pitches certainly helps.

However, this pressure to build a social audience and then extract value from it is where – as Simon Chambers, owner of Storm Management, says – several industries and professions are beginning to converge. One can see how important it has become in the entertainment sector as traditional celebrities and models rush to Instagram and YouTube to add the influencer string to their bow. Dickinson, who frequently works with people from both professions, says: 'There's no question celebrities and models are encouraged to build audiences on social media to get jobs.' She warns, though, that this is not always a good idea – not everyone who is a star on screen and in the pages of magazines is necessarily cut out to be an influencer. 'It really depends how real they are willing to be and how much their audience wants to see that,' she says. 'You have to work out if being transparent is going to work for you.'

Celebrities who have benefited from embracing the digital space include actor Busy Philipps who – thanks to utilizing Instagram Stories brilliantly in 2017 – became a bigger star online than she had on television or film and was given a late-night talk show by E!, *Busy Tonight*. Jack Black has a gaming YouTube channel, Will Smith is also creating regular high and low production value content for the platform and Jada Pinkett Smith provided Facebook Watch with her chat show *Red Table Talk*.

Dickinson cites Reese Witherspoon as a celebrity who is also using digital platforms and utilizing her influence there phenomenally well. 'You really get a sense of what she's about and I think what she's done with social media has released her. Her pictures are still beautiful but it feels authentic.'

Although Leona Farquharson – YouTube's global lead for top creators – cites prolific vloggers such as Liza Koshy as the 'heartbeat' of the platform, she highlights the desire for celebrities to engage directly with their fans and have creative control as a huge draw for more traditional talent. As a medium, Will Smith seems particularly suited to it, producing videos that include cameos from equally prolific stars as well as utilizing classic YouTube content formats such as Storytime. In the trailer for his channel, he says: 'I cannot believe how much YouTube has awakened me, I'm finding my voice and there's so much stuff I want to say.'

Spoken like a true influencer.

FIVE INFLUENCERS WORKING TO CHANGE THE WORLD

Gina Martin: a social activist whose eighteen-month campaign made the practice of upskirting – taking pictures of another person's genitals and underwear without their consent – illegal when the House of Lords approved a ban in 2019. Martin went on a mission to change the law after being a victim of upskirting while at a music festival in 2017 and being told by police there was nothing they could do to penalize the perpetrator.

Lola Omolola: a former journalist who founded Facebook group Female In Nigeria – now called Female IN – in 2015 after terrorist organization Boko Haram kidnapped 276 school girls in April 2014. This is a private group on the platform through which over one million women share issues they are facing as well as their experiences of sexual and domestic abuse in a safe space where religious advice and negative judgement are banned.

Kim Kardashian West: the reality star and entrepreneur met US president Donald Trump in 2018 to request he commute the sentence of great-grandmother Alice Marie Johnson, who was serving a life sentence for a non-violent drug crime. Johnson was released in that year. She has also advocated for Cyntoia Brown, a sex-trafficked child who was jailed for life after killing a man who had raped her.

Ed Winters: also known as Earthling Ed, Winters is a vegan and animal rights activist who engages in civil, compassionate debates with people working directly in the meat trade such as butchers and farmers and shares these discussions on his YouTube channel. He also organizes animal rights marches and is a frequent broadcaster on the realities of the agriculture industry.

DeRay Mckesson: a podcaster and civil rights activist, Mckesson supports the Black Lives Matter movement via protests and sharing news across Twitter and Instagram. He also presents Pod Save the People, a Crooked Media podcast about social justice through which he sheds light on local and national issues in America with experts and influencers.

USING INSTAGRAM FOR SOCIAL GOOD

FOR PHOTOGRAPHER ALICE AEDY, INSTAGRAM was never going to be a place for selfies and confessional monologues but she describes the direction her work has taken – using her platform to tell the stories of refugees – as something of an 'accident'. She says: 'I have always been fascinated by politics, humanitarian issues and my ability to make social impact.' A volunteering trip to the Calais Jungle refugee camp in 2016 set in motion a six-month stint of helping refugees during which she worked at another camp called Idomeni on the Greek–North Macedonian border where approximately 15,000 people were stuck due to the Balkan route being closed in March of the same year. 'I worked with a group of friends to cook 7,000 meals a day but always had a camera around my neck,' she says. Having seen journalists and photographers document the conditions of the camp and people living there, she recognized there was an opportunity for storytelling. 'This was at a time when people were using derogatory terms to talk about refugees,' she says, referencing former UK prime minister David Cameron's 'swarm of migrants' comment. 'I knew that given my close relationship with many of the families, I could play a role in taking images and sharing individual stories.' She started her Instagram account to publish the imagery and narratives she had gathered approximately a year later, having been inspired by a meeting with the founders of charity Help Refugees UK. 'I consider myself lucky to have grown up in a generation where I have been given the tools to shout loudly about the social issues, injustices and inequalities I am most passionate about,' she says.

Aedy is not just focused on telling the stories of displaced individuals with accuracy and respect, but also on the depiction of her subjects themselves. 'One thing I try to remember is to photograph subjects as if I was photographing my own friends or family,' she says. 'I think that level of respect is often forgotten for photojournalists who report abroad and neglect the power imbalance that can occur in the field.'

An example of this is a series of portraits she shot in Somaliland following the drought of 2017. These were taken in a portable studio – rather than on a backdrop of poverty and suffering – in order to separate the people as individuals with identities beyond the context they were in. She says: 'Photographing this way, we hoped to create a greater sense of connection with the subject and empathy on behalf of the viewer, while bringing attention back to Somaliland a year on from the worst of the drought.'

KEY TAKEAWAYS

- Generation Z will be trickier to work with as influencers because many produce content focusing on moral and social issues, rather than promoting consumerism and products. Some 26 per cent of individuals from this demographic in America alone admitted they will boycott a company if it supports values and practices at odds with their own. This may make brands re-examine their production processes down to their packaging choices as an imperative piece of work if they are to capture youth markets moving forward.
- The perfection-focused neatness, aspirational and staged content that has defined Instagram's first era is being abandoned by influencers focused on community-building as they have recognized their audience responds more passionately to candid imagery and raw dialogue about the realities of everyday life.
- Younger generations are turning the camera round and using social media to document issues they care about, rather than focusing their attention solely on their own lives. In addition, they are an 'ideas-focused' demographic for whom memes and jokes have more value than aspiration.
- The concept of what it means to be an influencer is rapidly changing due to celebrity adoption and utilization of digital platforms such as YouTube

194   INFLUENCE

to make independent content, through which they can talk to their
followers directly. In addition, people working in adjacent industries
such as modelling are being encouraged to develop their own audience;
bringing digital influence to the table of any project is seen as a huge
advantage.

- Businesses may have to deal with a ripple effect coming from how
influencers are redefining the workplace and expectations of what a
career can look like. While a linear path supported by 9:00 am–5:00 pm
hours is still by and large what most companies offer, influencers have
proved that a more plural approach through which they can explore
several passions is possible.

- Influencers who were significantly early adopters of social media and
independent content creation are moving towards a platform-agnostic
mindset, in which they are less concerned about which social networks
survive. They fully expect to continue publishing digital content
throughout their careers but – perhaps due to the quality of their
legacy – are not sentimental about where this happens. Second-
generation influencers, who have achieved success primarily through
Instagram, have a greater loyalty to the platform.

GLOSSARY OF INFLUENCER AND SOCIAL MEDIA TERMINOLOGY

As this book details, social media platforms are a world of their own and the influencers who dominate the different communities in each one have a language that reflects this. Here are some key terms, which are not only referenced in the preceding chapters, but are – in some cases – becoming part of everyday vernacular too.

Apology video created by YouTubers after a controversy that involves some kind of unacceptable behaviour from them. The production rate of apology videos was particularly high in 2018 following numerous uncoverings of historic tweets by influencers expressing discriminatory opinions and publishing videos that were culturally insensitive. Apology videos are now so part of YouTube culture that content creator Jack Douglass – also known as Jacksfilms – dressed up as an apology for Halloween 2018.

Cancelled the term applied to someone who has expressed discriminatory views – either presently or historically – or produced content that is culturally insensitive. This should not be taken literally as cancellations tend to last for a short period of time, during which an influencer may make their platforms private or release an apology video or tweet. Depending on the severity of the reason for the cancellation, this may not impact on influencers' current or future commercial partnerships.

Challenge a YouTube format that entertainment content creators tend to create videos based on while it is trending. Also, some challenge formats outlast the trend and become part of the YouTube landscape indefinitely. For example, 'Boyfriend does my ASOS shop' and 'Kids do the grocery shop'.

Chatty vlog similar to a personal update, in which a lifestyle YouTuber shares recent news with their subscribers, frequently while doing their make-up. These videos are always within familiar settings – the content creator's bedroom or living room, for example.

Clickbait misleading text or pictures specifically used to encourage users to click through to content. Clickbait is most frequently posted on Twitter and YouTube and often followed by disappointment.

Collab when two influencers work together on a piece of content which they cross-promote to both of their audiences. Popularized by early-adopting YouTubers who created a collab culture to accelerate their audience growth, but also a strategy used to great success by Instagram ecosystems. Works best when the collaborators are friends in real life too.

Daily vlog when an influencer posts a vlog every single day on YouTube, which documents their life. These often feature monotonous tasks such as going to the gym and grocery shopping, and some content creators also have secondary vlogging channels to host this content in one place. The practice of daily vlogging is often cited as a reason for YouTuber burnout.

Diss track a song intended to attack, insult or 'disrespect' another influencer. Popularized on YouTube between 2016 and 2017, the victim tends to create their own diss track in response.

Draw my life a video format in which the creator tells their life story through illustrations. Usually on YouTube.

Dying when one is in the process of having their mind blown due to shocking news or an incredible product. Used widely across all social media platforms.

Favourites a popular YouTube video format, usually created by lifestyle content creators on a monthly basis to highlight the most effective products they have used over the past four weeks. They also link to featured products in the caption below the video.

Flatlay a still-life shot for which an influencer will lay items that suggest an aspirational lifestyle – everything from make-up to books, sunglasses and coffee – on a blank background and aerially take a photograph of the composition. Most commonly found on Instagram.

Get ready with me (GRWM) a YouTube video format for which content creators film themselves choosing outfits and doing their make-up in preparation for an event, or day/night out. Found predominantly on YouTube.

Hate follow when someone follows an influencer on social media with the intention of trolling them because they do not enjoy their content or agree with their point of view.

Haul a video format in which the vlogger showcases the contents of a shopping spree either from a particular brand or across multiple ones but with a seasonal or specific focus, e.g. a winter haul or a make-up haul. Primarily found on YouTube and frequently referenced on Instagram and Twitter.

Hypebeast: refers to an individual who invests in and collects exclusive items from hyped streetwear and luxury brands. One of their primary concerns when shopping is the potential resale value of what they buy. This is not necessarily a complementary label but can often be used in a derogatory fashion.

I'm dead for when one's mind is blown. Used widely across all social media platforms.

Lightroom presets software developed by Adobe that allows influencers to quickly ensure all of their photography is edited in the same way, showcasing the same levels of colour saturation, shadow and light. Frequently used on Instagram. In addition, influencers sell packages of the presets levels they have created so that their followers can create pictures that look like theirs.

Memes humorous pictures and text that make observations on things that are relatable, culturally relevant or politically important.

Mukbang YouTube format popularized in South Korea in which a content creator eats an excessive amount of food while talking about their life.

Mylk a brand of coconut milk but also used to refer to plant-based milk in general. Used by vegan or plant-based vloggers/bloggers across Instagram and YouTube.

On fleek: to look on point or when part of one's appearance is exceptionally good. For example, "her eyebrows are on fleek". Used across YouTube, Instagram and Twitter.

OOTD (outfit of the day) can also be outfit of the night. Used primarily on Instagram but started as a fashion blogger content format.

Q&A a video format in which an influencer will answer questions from their followers that have been asked on Twitter, Snapchat or Instagram. This was originally popular on YouTube but is also frequently used on Instagram Stories.

Queen/qween refers to a person who is sassy, successful and confident.

Receipts to display evidence during an argument. For example: 'don't go there, I've got receipts'.

Shook used across all social platforms to express disbelief, anger or surprise.

Shooketh a step beyond shook. Used across all social platforms to express extreme disbelief, anger or surprise.

Sis/sisters a term used to identify female friends, but also used generally among beauty, black and LGBTQ+ communities. Sis is commonly used on Black Twitter and Sisters was popularized by beauty vlogger James Charles, who uses this word to refer collectively to his followers.

Salty to be bitter or jealous towards something or someone. Used across all platforms.

Slay to be on the top of one's game or to dominate. This is also used to compliment someone when they look brilliant. Originally used by LGBTQ+ community and Black Twitter, but popularized by Beyoncé with 'Formation', the first release from her 2016 album *Lemonade*.

Snatched this is similar to being on fleek and used when someone's outfit and make-up are looking particularly good. Typically used by beauty and LGBTQ+ vloggers. Made popular by television show *RuPaul's Drag Race*.

Snatch your wig/wig snatched refers to either someone blowing another person's mind (so that their wig falls off) or calling another out with evidence that proves them wrong. Again, made popular by television show *RuPaul's Drag Race* and commonly used on YouTube.

Spill the tea/T refers to an influencer revealing gossip or the truth. Originated from the drag community in San Antonio, Texas, but is now popular in America and Britain across YouTube, Instagram and Twitter.

Squad a group of friends collectively supporting each other's success. Popularized on Instagram by Taylor Swift in 2015 through the video for her single 'Bad Blood'.

Storytime a YouTube video format in which a content creator dramatically retells an interesting or curious event. Often very juicy.

Unboxing a video format in which vloggers unveil items they have either been sent or have purchased from their packaging. Popularized on YouTube, but now also used on Instagram albeit in a short form which is all show and no tell.

VidCon a YouTuber conference founded in 2010 by writers, content creators and brothers Hank and John Green, known for their channel Vlog Brothers. They sold the event to Viacom in 2018. Originally held in Southern California, this is now becoming a global event where influencers from across all genres gather to take part in panel discussions and meet with fans.

Vlog YouTube's equivalent of a blog post (video blog).

Vlogmas a vlogging challenge in which participants film a video every single day between 1 December and Christmas Eve. Mostly Christmas themed, but not necessarily. Exclusive to YouTube.

Yass variation of 'yes' used as an exclamation of support and excitement for another person. Made popular by drag queens and the LGBTQ+ community but now used across mainstream media.

INDEX